THE
PROPHETIC
PERSPECTIVE

THE
PROPHETIC
PERSPECTIVE

Seeing and Seizing Our God-Intended Future

mark chironna

DESTINY IMAGE. PUBLISHERS, INC.

P.O. Box 310, Shippensburg, PA 17257-0310

"Promoting Inspired Lives."

This book and all other Destiny Image, Revival Press, MercyPlace, Fresh Bread, Destiny Image Fiction, and Treasure House books are available at Christian bookstores and distributors worldwide.

For a U.S. bookstore nearest you, call 1-800-722-6774.

For more information on foreign distributors, call 717-532-3040.

Reach us on the Internet: www.destinyimage.com.

ISBN 13 TP: 978-0-7684-4212-0

ISBN 13 Ebook: 978-0-7684-8734-3

For Worldwide Distribution, Printed in the U.S.A.

1 2 3 4 5 6 7 8 / 17 16 15 14 13

Endorsements

Mark Chironna does an outstanding job of laying out biblical exegesis of the position and purpose of the church, the apostle, and the prophet. He brings clarity and doctrinal balance to the prophetic foundation of the Body of Christ. He masterfully weaves between the Old and New Covenants to demonstrate God's prophetic intent for our lives. I highly recommend this book.

Dr. Ché Ahn
Senior Pastor, HROCK Church, Pasadena, California
President, Harvest International Ministry
International Chancellor, Wagner Leadership Institute

The body of Christ has been waiting for this book! Dr. Chironna has written an in-depth biblical exposition on the five-fold ministry gift of the prophet. This is the most thoughtful, scriptural throughout, and prophetically insightful examination of the ministry of the prophet I've ever read! Dr. Chironna's powerful prophetic ministry has had a tremendous impact on my life. He is a well-respected, beyond reproach, world-class prophet of God who has written to us what he has lived in ministry for decades. I've often admired Dr. Chironna for his incredible intellect, and as I read through this amazing book, it became very apparent why the Lord would ask him to write this for us. His unique insights are based on extensive biblical study coupled with incredible prophetic insight, which culminates in giving us one of the most profound studies on the prophet ever written.

This is the book we've all been waiting for on the ministry of the prophet. Thank you, Dr. Chironna, for giving God's people this great gift!

DR. MICHAEL MAIDEN

Dr. Mark Chironna is one of the greatest communicators of our day. He has a unique ability to help unlock your personal destiny and help us as a church discover where we are, so we can get to where God wants us to be! This book is full of powerful prophetic insights and is a must read for every believer!

MARTHA MUNIZZI
Award-Winning Singer/Songwriter
International Praise and Worship Leader

Dr. Chironna's book *The Prophetic Perspective* really hits the nail on the head. It outlines the proper attitude and motivation we should all be pressing into concerning the prophetic anointing. This important book shares the intent of the Father in prophetic operation, sharing what to avoid, what to pursue, and key points for activating the godly perspective of prophecy in the church and in the individual. It's these kinds of books that supercharge the reader, imparting an element of Christ's grace and anointing in their lives and ministries, and teach us all how not to squander the precious resources of the Lord.

JAMES MALONEY
Author, *The Dancing Hand of God* and *The Panoramic Seer*

In an age of revisionism and relativism, Mark's book *The Prophetic Perspective* has much to say about the consistent Kingdom role of the prophet in a constantly changing world.

Real prophets rise above logic and rationale to bring an intuition from another dimension. Prophets hear the voice of God, see the hand of God, and know the times of God. This is a valuable tool in understanding the ways of a prophet in the context of revealing the Kingdom.

GRAHAM COOKE
brilliantbookhouse.com

What does *that* mean? What was *that*? If you haven't asked these questions, you just haven't been to a Spirit-filled church! In his latest book, *The Prophetic Perspective: Seeing and Seizing Our God-Intended Future*, Dr. Mark Chironna will lead you through a biblical understanding of what all things prophetic mean so you will never have to ask the *that* question.

DR. SAMUEL R. CHAND
Author of *Cracking Your Church's Culture Code*
www.samchand.com

This is a much-needed book, bringing clarity in the midst of a plethora of prophetic ideologies that at times are confusing and others even deceptive, some even false. Mark Chironna lays a great foundation for prophets and the prophetic, embracing their value as well as taking us back to first things regarding the prophetic. He demystifies and recenters this God-given gift and office to the church. The Word and the Church!

BARBARA YODER

Mark Chironna has produced a vital book for the times in which we live. As a proven prophet for many years, Mark writes from experience as well as from a wealth of knowledge. God has declared that He will do nothing on earth without first revealing it to His prophets. The truths within this book can revolutionize your life and help you discover your prophetic destiny.

DR. BILL HAMON
Bishop of Christian International Ministries Network (CIMN, VCCI)
Christian International Apostolic Network, CI Global Network
Author of 12 major books, such as *Prophets and Personal Prophecy* and
Apostles, Prophets, and the Coming Moves of God

As a great ambassador for Christ, Dr. Mark Chironna raises the standard for us on what a true prophetic ministry looks like and what a true prophet today is to exemplify. Taking us on a journey of both Old and New Testament examples, Mark leads us on an adventure that is both exhilarating and fulfilling. He points us to the Word, he points us to character, and he points us to our upward call in Christ Jesus. Be inspired as you read about God's eternal purpose and step into it for yourself!

Dr. James W. Goll

Encounters Network, Prayer Storm, Compassion Acts

Author of *The Seer, Dream Language, The Lost Art of Intercession, The Lost Art of Pure Worship*, and many more.

The prophet Joel spoke of a last days' spiritual downpour that would become a supernatural deluge, drenching even the least likely, the disqualified, and the disenfranchised. This heavy rain would manifest in a flood of prophetic ministry that would be unrivaled in human history. In the midst of this outpouring, tares would take root in society. False prophets masquerading as the real deal would threaten to infest the entire field of dreams with deception. But God had a strategic plan to raise up true prophets who would equip an entire generation of saints. This prophetic army would unmask deceivers and release a pristine river of prophetic clarity into the earth.

Today we find ourselves right in the middle of Joel's river of revelation. The Holy Spirit is falling on people all over the world, which is creating a desperate need for prophetic fathers and mothers to train, equip, and deploy a mighty army and send them into the fray.

Mark Chironna is one of the most masterfully skilled prophets of our time. His manuscript, entitled *Prophetic Perspective: Seeing and Seizing Our God-Intended Future,* is more than a book. It's a field-training manual for multitudes of people who find themselves awakened to new spiritual dimensions and yet struggle to navigate the white waters of supernatural power. Mark's book is full of fatherly insights and godly wisdom. *Prophetic Perspective* will direct the misguided, inspire the disheartened, clarify the confused, and empower the masses. I highly recommend this book to everyone in this outpouring.

Kris Vallotton

Co-Founder of Bethel School of Supernatural Ministry

Author of eight books including

The Supernatural Ways of Royalty and *Spirit Wars*

Leader, Bethel Church, Redding, California

"And the prophets of God were with them, helping them" (Ezra 5:2 NIV). The prophetic ministry is often misused. Certainly, it is also misunderstood. But, the prophetic is integral to the health and forward movement of the church. We live in a time of spiritual confusion and ever-shifting values that seek to move us further and further off course. We need prophetic clarity more than ever. Thank you, Dr. Chironna, for a great resource to help the church to more fully understand and appreciate this vital ministry.

MIKE SERVELLO
Founding Pastor, Redeemer Church
Founder, Compassion Coalition

Mark's brilliant work, *The Prophetic Perspective: Seeing and Seizing Our God-Intended Future*, is so desperately needed at this present time. The way that Mark explains the ascension gifts and the fact that God gave these as gifts so that we can be built up in love is of paramount importance. The ascension gifts are not curses but blessings to His people. Mark's deep understanding of *kairos* makes this book stand out above all books written on the prophetic. I know the importance of timing. Could it be that Mark has done exactly that? This book, written at the right moment in time, could lead you not only to a powerful word but to a *powerful event*. This insightful book will give you an exegesis of existence from a divine perspective and move you from zero to hero. How? *Read the book!* You'll never be the same. Welcome to the future.

KIM CLEMENT

Dr. Mark Chironna is one of a handful of people with whom I have casual conversations—and wish they were recorded after I hang up. This book is like a conversation with Dr. Mark, pregnant with insight after insight, page after page. He will not only upgrade your perception about all things operating under the banner of "prophetic" but all things vital to your own unique one of a kind calling and destiny will be clearer than ever before. Some books you buy to read later; this is a book to buy, read, and enjoy *now*.

LANCE WALLNAU
Director, Lance Learning Group

Contents

Foreword

Dr. Mark Chironna has written another masterpiece. His profound yet practical insights, coupled with his writing skills, make this book an exciting journey. I was already hooked just reading the introduction. It is encouraging to read something about the prophetic that is neither reactionary nor careless in creating "new truth." The *Prophetic Perspective: Seeing and Seizing Our God-Intended Future* disarms the cautious reader with unusual wisdom on a sensitive but important subject. Dr. Chironna explains the role and purpose of the prophet through solid biblical study while also embracing the thrilling moving of the Spirit. And that is quite an accomplishment. Each of us has a role in the unfolding plan of God for this planet. In the final pages of this book we come to God's invitation to intimacy that releases transformation to the world around us. This book captures the core and purpose of the prophetic and gives us clarity of our role in seeing reformation in our lifetime.

BILL JOHNSON
Senior Pastor of Bethel Church, Redding, California
Author of *When Heaven Invades Earth* and
Hosting the Presence

Introduction

The prophetic purpose is much more radical than social change... —WALTER BRUEGGEMANN, The Prophetic Imagination[1]

IF ASKED, MANY FOLLOWERS OF CHRIST WOULD SAY THEY ATTEND A prophetic church, have traveled to a prophetic conference, or have been impacted by the ministry of a prophet. In some circles, it is common to say, "Our worship team moves in the prophetic," or "Sister Sally received her mantle at Brother Elijah's Prophetic Academy," or "That prophet had *a word* tonight!"

As relevant as it is to the Body of Christ, the word *prophetic* has become, to some, a catch phrase. Often the term is used to cover spiritual activity that is difficult to describe or classify. It is applied to experiences that seem to be more than the "usual" or to forms of ministry that reach more deeply into the heart and soul of the saint. Some refer to the prophetic when describing something that is new or unfamiliar.

If pressed to explain further, would they—or we—be able to explain what the word *prophetic* really means? The question is not rhetorical but practical. Even as you read this sentence, the realm of the prophetic is being discussed in the four corners of the 21st-century Church. The fact that it is being discussed is good; the reality that it is viewed in wildly divergent and often tentative ways is, in part, the reason this book was written.

My point is not that diversity in the Body of Christ is suspect but that the prophetic need not be mysterious, confusing, or a source of contention. Along the way, you have probably seen evidence of it being all three. In some quarters, the prophetic is discussed as a kind of ecclesiastical curiosity, something that happens "somewhere, but not here." In many pews and pulpits, mere talk of the prophetic denotes a cult underfoot. In other sectors, the prophetic is seen as an essential element of church life that enriches the spiritual walks of those who embrace it; and in some, the prophetic label sparks a note of elitism.

From every angle, the prophetic is a hot topic. Christian booksellers line their shelves with prophetic titles. Bible studies keep the dialogue open, and often fiery. Apostles, prophets, and other members of the fivefold ministry strive to clarify muddy waters and address misguided quests for spiritual goose bumps. Pastors guard their sheep, rightly warding off prophetic dilettantes and sometimes inadvertently barring the ministry of God-sent ones whose callings and election are sure.

To approach the prophetic with gravitas is appropriate. To embrace its authentic manifestations is equally important. Prophetic expression is not a matter of religious curiosity but of spiritual genetics; it was mapped in the DNA of the Church by our Creator. Throughout the millennia, prophets have played a vital role in the unfolding of God's eternal purpose. Prophetic acts and utterances are described throughout Scripture and continue to inform the workings of the Church of Jesus Christ as she fulfills her role in God's ultimate plan of redemption and restoration.

Through the context of redemptive history, we will see that the truly prophetic is as real and God-honoring today as it was in Old-Testament times. In the coming pages, we will uncover our prophetic roots and explore the big picture of God's purposes in this age. Three questions underlie our study:

1. What is the prophetic, and what are the hallmarks of the genuine article?

2. What are the outcomes effected by authentic prophet-
    ic ministry?

3. How are we to steward this aspect of spiritual life, individ-
    ually and as the Body?

These questions and their implications are weighty because they demand careful consideration of God's intent. They also force us to reckon with what we believe or tacitly accept as being true. Doctrinal boundaries may be tested along the way; you may find yourself in complete agreement at one point and at odds the next. The process is not meant to be an affront, although by dint of the subject matter, offense may tug at your soul. Some will be sur-prised to find that *we* are the offended ones—even momentarily—when we stumble across *our* sacred cows and see them in a new, uncomfortable light.

Discomfort may be an unavoidable part of our prophetic study, yet the intent is positive: First, to raise questions that test our notions of funda-mental truths; second, to promote unity in the Body of Christ; and third, to encourage the Church to operate in the fullness of her calling in this pivotal age.

Who Are We?

We will consider our three underlying questions from a variety of plat-forms and with a snapshot of today's Church in mind. Before we frame our snapshot, we need to establish some Scriptural baselines. One is the apostle Paul's inspired characterization of the Church of Jesus Christ:

> *So then you are no longer strangers and aliens, but you are fellow citizens with the saints, and are of **God's household,** having been **built upon the foundation of the apostles and proph-ets, Christ Jesus Himself being the corner stone,** in whom the whole building, being fitted together is growing into a holy temple in the Lord; in whom you also are being built together into a dwelling of God in the Spirit* (Ephesians 2:19-22).

Paul's words are threaded with spiritual identity markers. He explains that we are not outsiders but members of a spiritual household—*the* spiritual household for all eternity. Our assignments are unique and cause us to fit together in the matrix of divine purpose. *Yes!* Each of our lives is meaningful because it is uniquely fashioned by God!

Because these truths are at the crux of everything God's people are and do, Paul's words will come up often in our discussion. As we begin our journey, three points are key:

1. *The household of God is dynamic.* Ephesians 2:22 says that we are *"being built together into a dwelling of God in the Spirit."* This building process is ongoing. We are not so much *building* as *being built.* God's structure could not be conceived or erected by human design. Neither can it be sustained by human works. We are being built by God Himself, with His eternal purpose in mind. Our part is to cooperate with Him, in the Spirit.

2. *God's household has been built upon a particular foundation.* Ephesians 2:20 describes it as a *"foundation of the apostles and prophets."* Interestingly, there is no mention of the remaining fivefold ministry offices of evangelist, pastor, and teacher (see Eph. 4:11-12). The construction of the foundation is important; the right foundation lends strength and enhances function. This is certainly true of the Church that is, even now, *"growing into a holy temple in the Lord."*

3. *Jesus Christ is the Chief Cornerstone.* He is our center of gravity in all things, the mortar in our structure, and the source of all we are called to be and do. The Chief Cornerstone binds together all other stones—the members of Christ's Body whom Peter described as *"living stones,* [who] *are being built up as a spiritual house for a holy priesthood, to offer up spiritual sacrifices acceptable to God through Jesus Christ"* (1 Pet. 2:5).

Another aspect of our New Testament identity was disclosed by Peter who said, *"It is you who are the sons of the prophets, and of the covenant which God made with your fathers, saying to Abraham, 'And in your seed all the families of the earth shall be blessed'"* (Acts 3:25). We will explore the implications of Peter's words in later chapters. Suffice to say for now that we are the sons and daughters of the prophets, the seed of Abraham, and the children and beneficiaries of the covenant God made with the father of the faith.

Although we are the spiritual descendants of the prophets who came before us, New Covenant prophets are not entirely modeled after the lineage beginning with Abraham and ending with John the Baptist. Old Covenant prophets operated in a different arena from Ephesians 4:11 prophets. The prophets who minister at your church will not find their words being added to canon the way Isaiah's and Jeremiah's were. Nor will modern prophets foretell the first coming of the Messiah as those before Christ did. Instead, the New Covenant prophet is one sent by Christ *"for the equipping of the saints for the work of service, to the building up of the body of Christ..."* (Eph. 4:12). The New Covenant prophet is of a different order and follows a post-ascension template.

One more point of clarification: many interpret canon to say that the tongues (and other gifts) first seen on the Day of Pentecost and elsewhere in the New Testament have ceased. I find no biblical support for this position. In fact, Peter preached in Acts 3 as one who was baptized in the Holy Spirit. He was one of 120 in the Upper Room who declared the wonderful works of God. So the "sons of the prophets" are more accurately described as *the Church baptized in the Holy Spirit.*

Now for our snapshot.

Where Are We?

The Church is a supernatural entity unlike any in our world. Despite her failures and missteps, untold testimonies reverberate through the household of God—stories of indescribable miracles, life transformations, and global impact. The Church's significant strengths flow from the Chief Cornerstone and work through those who are *in Him* (see Rom. 12:5; 1 Pet. 5:14).

Because our purpose is to advance His cause, we are also called to judge ourselves honestly. We must be quick to identify our weaknesses and eager to know what they reveal about our alignment with God's eternal purpose.

We know in the most general sense that the world is moving the way it has since the Fall of Man—with no conscious awareness of God's eternal purpose being wrought in the earth. Absent this awareness, the world is naturally predisposed to resisting God's intent. Because it is comprised of human beings, the Church experiences similar areas of misalignment. When John wrote the Book of Revelation, it was sent, not to the world, but to God's called-out company. It is startling to note that the resurrected Christ assessed most of the Church in Asia Minor to be in decline—mere decades after His ascension. He warned the Church, saying: *"He who has an ear, let him hear what the Spirit says to the churches...."* (Rev. 2:7).

Signs of Decline

The decline of the Church did not catch Jesus by surprise in the first century, and it won't now. As the writer of Hebrews explained, *"We do not have a high priest who cannot sympathize with our weaknesses, [we have] One who has been tempted in all things as we are, yet without sin"* (Heb. 4:15). Our Savior loves us enough to expose our flaws to His light so that we can address them. The following are some of key signs of decline in our modern age:

Doctrinal Drift

Jesus' words to the early Church should command our attention today. On a macro level, errant and even blatantly false doctrines have infiltrated Church ranks. Among these is universalism. While the biblical view of salvation rests in justification *by faith* in the finished work of Christ, universalism asserts that all people will ultimately be saved because all are predestined for redemption.

Another notable shift is the belief that we have already entered the Kingdom age. This line of reasoning asserts that the Church has been replaced by the Kingdom in God's agenda. The question is: How can we separate the Church and the Kingdom when Jesus did not do so? He said that the Kingdom was at hand even as the Church was about to be birthed (see Matt. 4:17; 10:7; Mark 1:15).

A third example of errant doctrine is the Emergent Church Movement, which skirts the issue of sin and dilutes foundational truths, such as Bible inerrancy. This approach highlights God's grace but fails to disclose that our loving Savior endorsed the commands of Scripture, saying: *"Do not think that I came to abolish the Law or the Prophets; I did not come to abolish, but to fulfill"* (Matt. 5:17).

On the opposite end of the spectrum from Emergent Church philosophy is the stringency of legalism, which encourages followers to earn their salvation, as though holiness were achieved through performance and not grace. Legalism focuses on the outward man or woman to such a degree as to forget that God is concerned with the condition of the heart. Romans 2:29 refers to true circumcision as being inward: *"that which is of the heart, by the Spirit, not by the letter; and his praise is not from men, but from God."*

The Superficial Church

Church decline can also be seen in an overemphasis on church size. Instead of focusing on the integrity of the foundation (made of apostles and prophets) and the mission to make disciples, some church leaders approach their stewardship as a franchise-type operation geared to attracting the masses. It is not necessarily the business structure that taints; every church needs a well-functioning structure. The distortion enters when churches are thought to be validated by prescribed growth patterns. Preoccupation with numbers makes seeker-friendly formats attractive. Often, the quest for popularity trumps the bearing of truth—in the local community, among visitors, and within the larger Christian community.

A natural outgrowth of this business "model" and a recurring characteristic overall is the tendency for churches to become spiritual social clubs, something churches were never called to be. Instead of being salt and light to their communities, churches end up promoting names and events. It as though God's purpose is not to draw people to Himself but to personalities and experiences. Celebrity culture (disguised as Kingdom expansion) and the desire of church attenders to be entertained serve hand in glove to breed theological shallowness. Paul warned of this tendency:

> For the time will come when they will not endure sound doctrine; but wanting to have their ears tickled, they will accumulate for themselves teachers in accordance to their own desires... (2 Timothy 4:3).

The shallow state is diametrically opposed to Christ's intent to *"fill all things"* (Eph. 4:10). It reduces the Christian walk to a series of formulas, confessions, and Scripture memorizations that require no critical thinking or depth of relationship with Christ. Shallowness suppresses any appetite for the strong meat of the Word (see Heb. 5:12-14) while simultaneously nourishing a drift from sound doctrine. Instead of worshiping God in spirit and truth (see John 4:24), believers end up worshiping the latest revelation and those who deliver it.

It is easy to see how these tendencies stunt spiritual growth and maturity and render churches ineffective. Instead of feasting on a diet of transforming truths, attendees snack on sermonettes. As a result, the nature of covenant is misunderstood and basics such as tithing are cast off and even derided as being old-fashioned or out of touch.

These symptoms reveal an ailment that is eating away at many churches: it is the disconnect from God's intentionality in filling all things in Christ (see Eph. 4:10). Where the ailment goes untreated, churches become Christian ghettos in which believers focus on self, seek after signs, and fail to transform the world outside their doors.

The Echo Chamber

The message of the Church is the testimony of Jesus Christ: He died. He was buried. He was raised on the third day, after leading captivity captive (see Ps. 68:18 NKJV; Eph. 4:8 NKJV). And—hallelujah!—He will come again.

As followers of Christ, we *believe* this and declare it to be so. These are the truths we ratified in our hearts when we accepted Him as Savior and Lord. Oddly enough, the unanimity of the true Church in this regard may help to explain a subtle weakness seen throughout the Body—namely, a sense of familiarity that manifests in several ways.

If you have been in the Church any length of time—and especially if you are a new believer—you are aware of the Christian dialect. Every Christian stream has its own lingo. Buzz words emerge and become passkeys to facilitate and affirm our shared beliefs and experiences. Lingo is a unifying element in any community. The danger is not in the vocabulary but in the degree to which we unconsciously regurgitate ideas and internalize "scripts" without questioning or understanding them. Even Scripture, our fundamental unifying language, can become so familiar as to be tuned out.

We have all been there: John 3:16 is read and our eyes glaze over. The unconscious mind declares: "I already know *that.*" This response inoculates us against the impact and enormity of God's truth. The learning switch flips to the "off" position and we become spiritual know-it-alls—unteachable experts so familiar with God's Word that fresh fruit cannot be manifested in our lives. His stated purpose of *"growing* [us] *into a holy temple"* that is *"fitted together"* (Eph. 2:21) is neutralized and the Church becomes little more than a spiritual echo chamber.

re·duc·tion·ism

"The practice of simplifying a complex idea, issue, condition, or the like, especially to the point of minimizing, obscuring, or distorting it."[2]

Theologians have a name for this malady: it is called *reductionism.* In an age when Bible teaching is available 24 hours per day via cable, satellite, radio, podcast, broadcast television, and the Internet, it is easy to embrace the mistaken belief that we know it all. We unwittingly reduce truth to formulaic frozen meals we can store and reheat as needed. Self-satisfied and well-stocked with truth, we lose sight of our need and grow cold in our hearts. When the pastor speaks of sin, we assume the admonition is for someone else. We pat ourselves on the back and order the sermon CD for someone who doesn't know as much as we do.

Reductionism is costly: the more we think we know, the less God reveals. Sometimes, the very answer we seek is drowned out by the white noise of the echo chamber. Matthew 13:15 describes the problem and the price:

> *For the heart of this people has become dull, and with their ears they scarcely hear, and they have closed their eyes lest they should see with their eyes, and hear with their ears, and understand with their heart and return, and I would heal them.*

Sometimes, the very answer we seek is drowned out by the white noise of the echo chamber.

Pride Versus Grace

In his Bible paraphrase known as *The Message*, biblical scholar Eugene Peterson renders a well-known passage in an unforgettable way:

> *Are you tired? Worn out? Burned out on religion? Come to Me. Get away with Me and you'll recover your life. I'll show you how to take a real rest. Walk with Me and work with Me—watch how I do it.* **Learn the unforced rhythms of grace.** *I won't lay anything heavy or ill-fitting on you. Keep company with Me and you'll learn to live freely and lightly* (Matthew 11:28-30 MSG).

"Unforced rhythms of grace." The phrase evokes the unbounded freedom Christ offers. Though the life of faith has its challenges, the cross did not purchase a brand-new life of drudgery. Instead, Jesus continues to offer relief to the "*weary and heavy-laden*" (Matt. 11:28). He is aware of our inclination toward self-effort. He knows how unnatural it is for us to abandon our performance orientation, even after His finished work rendered our own works counterproductive. The apostle Paul addressed the issue in his letter to the Galatians:

> *Did you receive the Spirit by the works of the Law, or by hearing with faith? Are you so foolish? Having begun by the Spirit, are you now being perfected by the flesh?* (Galatians 3:2-3)

Among the world's weary and heavy-laden souls are those who seek recognition through self-righteousness. Two thousand years after Paul's epistle, and hundreds of years after the Reformation, much of the Church is *still* trying to fulfill His will through works of the flesh. Instead of simply yielding and allowing the Holy Spirit to work through us, we frustrate His grace by trying to prove that we are good enough and can achieve enough. In reality, we try to redeem ourselves.

Afraid to be seen as "less than" perfect (remember that our imperfection is the very reason Christ died for us), we slip into a brand of pride known as false humility. We try and try to please God and to reflect Him in our *doing*. Instead He desires that we release *His* power by simply *being* His children—bought, paid for, and humbled by His love. As long as we choose the forced rhythms of our own works, we are disqualified from entering the glory of His. Jesus revealed as much when He said, *"I praise Thee, O Father, Lord of heaven and earth, that Thou didst hide these things from the wise and intelligent and didst reveal them to infants"* (Matt. 11:25).

Where Is God Leading Us?

To understand where God is leading the Church, we need to establish two basic but profound points. The first point involves the message of the Church, which is the testimony of Jesus Christ. For 2,000 years, the message has been heralded; but in some quarters, liberties have been taken, and the authentic message must be recovered.

Recovery of the Testimony

It may surprise you to hear that the testimony of Jesus Christ is not the foremost message in every church that names Him. All streams of Christianity have produced pockets of overemphasis on something other than the pure testimony of Christ. It may be a fixation on signs and wonders, a preoccupation with the handling of snakes, a social gospel, such as liberation theology, or any of the doctrinal divergences already mentioned. The bottom line is this: wherever and to whatever degree *any* message is elevated above the testimony of Christ (God's *intended* message for the Church), God will lead us to recover the testimony in its entirety.

Just as He addressed the seven churches in the days of John the Beloved (see Rev. 2-3), He addresses us today and re-centers us on our first love (see Rev. 2:4). One of the primary means of testimony recovery is the ministry of the prophets whose job it is to assess the condition of the Church.

Alignment With God's Intent

Our second point involves the fact that God is intentional, while we tend to be fickle. We will discuss God's intentionality more in coming chapters; for now we need to establish the fact that His intentions are unwavering. When *we* waver, He calls us back on track—*His* track—and shows us how to recapture His intent. We need not wander from it, even accidentally; we need only ask the Holy Spirit to impress His intent upon us so we can become as deliberate about His Kingdom business as He is.

Many elements of His intent have already been revealed in Scripture. For example, we know that God intends for all things to be summed up in Christ (see Eph. 1:10). We also know that He intends for the Body of Christ to be *"fitted and held together by that which every joint supplies, according to the proper working of each individual part..."* (Eph. 4:16). He has already declared His desire for His *"manifold wisdom... [to] be made known through the church to the rulers and the authorities in the heavenly places"* (Eph. 3:10).

Whether we get on board with God or not, His intent is backed by divine purpose and *will be* accomplished. The question is whether we will choose to cooperate. It is the same challenge faced centuries ago, when Mordecai learned that Haman, an enemy of the Jews, had secured permission from King Ahasuerus to destroy the Jewish people (see Esther 3 and 4). Because Esther, Mordecai's cousin, was Ahasuerus' queen, Mordecai asked her to *"implore* [the king's] *favor and to plead with him for her people"* (Esther 4:8).

Esther had a lot on the line. She knew that approaching the king without being summoned by him would risk her favored position and even her life (see Esther 4:11). But as one of God's covenant people, she was uniquely situated to make a difference, and even to affect history. Mordecai saw Esther's predicament plainly and reminded her that, because of her Jewish heritage, her life was already in jeopardy (see Esther 4:13). Esther stood to lose everything whether she acted or not.

Mordecai stripped the dilemma of its horns with his unforgettable words:

> *If you remain silent at this time, relief and deliverance will arise for the Jews from another place and you and your father's house will perish. And who knows whether you have not attained royalty for such a time as this?* (Esther 4:14)

Conviction came by way of truth and brought Esther into alignment with her assignment. She agreed to risk everything and make God's eternal purpose her own. As a result, Haman was executed, Mordecai was promoted to second in command under the king, Esther continued her reign as queen, and God's people were preserved. God's intent was accomplished through the obedience of a woman who chose to answer His call, in His timing, whatever the cost.

There was a moment of truth when God's intent became Esther's. It was the moment when she said: *"...I will go in to the king...and if I perish, I perish"* (Esther 4:16).

An "Esther mentality" will serve the modern Church well in the fulfillment of her calling. It requires us to be humble and teachable, positioned to hear His voice and embrace His intent rather than our own. It also means recognizing our standing as God's covenant people—those grounded in the blessings and sanctions of covenant life. Once the glories of God's covenant become wedded to our identity as a Body, we will desire nothing less than He desires. Counterfeits will lose their appeal; celebrity culture and coddling messages will fall by the wayside.

Steadfastness

He is also leading us to become a steadfast people, not *"tossed here and there by waves, and carried about by every wind of doctrine, by the trickery of men, by craftiness in deceitful scheming..."* (Eph. 4:14), but rooted and grounded in God's intent, as Paul was. The apostle endured being whipped, beaten with rods, stoned, shipwrecked; he weathered dangerous journeys, persecution, sleep deprivation, hunger, thirst, and exposure to the elements (see 2 Cor. 11:24-29). With so many impediments against him, what was on Paul's mind? It was his *"concern for all the churches"* (2 Cor. 11:28).

Even when he knew imprisonment and death awaited him, Paul remained determined to preach the Gospel and finish his course (see Acts 20:24). Paul was not concerned with physical comforts or the desire to be recognized for his anointing or revelation; he was consumed with the desire to know Christ (see Phil. 3:8). Under the utmost pressure, the apostle *"did not shrink from declaring...the whole purpose of God"* (Acts 20:27).

Lordship and Liberty

God is leading the Church to be balanced in all things—neither caught in legalism nor careless with grace. The mature Church moves in grace's unforced rhythms (see Matt. 11:29 MSG), wading deeply into the liberty Jesus purchased for her at Calvary. Yet, freedom must be balanced with the very thing that made it possible: His Lordship. Second Corinthians 3:17 states plainly that *"the Lord is the Spirit; and where the Spirit of the Lord is, there is liberty."* There can be no liberty without the Lordship of Jesus Christ!

We have been freed not to build our kingdoms but to partake in the building of His. To rise to the challenge, we must proclaim our only message—the testimony of Jesus Christ. Our focus—if it is consecrated to His Lordship—is not on buildings, seating, social agendas, competition, sound systems, titles, or recognition, but on Him. Like Paul, we are called to the *"whole purpose of God"* (Acts 20:27).

The testimony of the Chief Cornerstone and a reverence for His Lordship will release the Church into new realms of freedom—not a rollercoaster ride of highs and lows, but a state of perpetual revival. The day is coming when the Church will be without *"spot or wrinkle"* (Eph. 5:27) and rightly consumed with talking about Him.

That is where the ministry of the prophet begins and ends.

Chapter 1

Covenant Harmony

The Lord your God will raise up for you a prophet like me from among you, from your countrymen, you shall listen to Him (DEUTERONOMY 18:15).

IT IS SUCH A SIMPLE SENTENCE, SUCH A FIRM AND FATHERLY COMMAND. Moses told the still-wandering Israelites: "Keep your eyes open because a prophet is coming. He will be like me, and you will listen to Him" (see Deut. 18:15, above).

The most significant prophet until the advent of Christ taught the Israelites to expect their Messiah, though His appearing was centuries away. Moses described the promised One; he planted in Israel's heart a picture they could understand: "He will be *like me*." Although they would not live in the flesh to witness the day of His coming, Moses imprinted the Messiah's identity on the collective consciousness of a nation.

Centuries later, Peter and John ministered healing to a lame man at the Gate Beautiful. Afterward, Peter explained the miracle to stunned witnesses (see Acts 3:1-18). To whet their spiritual appetites, Peter invoked the God of Abraham, Isaac, and Jacob and explained that faith in His glorified Son was what healed the lame man. Peter then served the entrée: he reminded the

Jews that the Son (the Messiah) had been prophesied to Israel. Peter continued his testimony of the Christ:

> Therefore repent and return, so that your sins may be wiped away, in order that times of refreshing may come from the presence of the Lord; and that He may send Jesus, the Christ appointed for you, whom heaven must receive until the period of restoration of all things about which God spoke by the mouth of His holy prophets from ancient time. Moses said, **"The Lord God shall raise up for you a prophet like me from your brethren; to Him you shall give heed in everything He says to you."** And it shall be that every soul that does not heed that prophet shall be utterly destroyed from among the people. And likewise, all the prophets who have spoken, from Samuel and his successors onward, also announced these days. It is you who are the sons of the prophets, and of the covenant which God made with your fathers, saying to Abraham, "And in your seed all the families of the earth shall be blessed." For you first, God raised up His Servant, and sent Him to bless you by turning every one of you from your wicked ways (Acts 3:19-26).

Standing on the opposite shore of Calvary from where Moses had stood, Peter confirmed that Jesus was *the* Prophet—the Messiah—to whom Moses had referred. All along, Israel had expected the Prophet to set people free. After all, He would be like Moses, and Moses was a deliverer. They had watched, fasted, and prayed for generations, with no sign of Messiah's appearance. Now, suddenly, Peter answered the question wrapped deep in their souls, saying, "This is the One you have been expecting."

Imagine the immensity of the moment!

Scripture or Prophecy?

Scripture had sustained the Jews' hopes for the Deliverer. The prophetic books promised His coming. But in reality, all of Scripture had foreshadowed Him. Because we tend, by nature, to categorize things, we also compartmentalize Scripture. We label certain books *prophetic* because they foretell things to come. Isaiah's description of the Suffering Servant in Isaiah 53 is a prime example of prophecy. Isaiah pointed God's people toward the Messiah who would come *someday*.

We label all the books of the Bible in various ways: we call them Wisdom books or Epistles or Gospels or Torah, and so on. While these categories are useful, they obscure the fact that *all Scripture is prophecy*. Did you catch that? *All Scripture is prophecy.*

It may be easier to believe this statement when you are reading Jeremiah and more difficult when you are in Leviticus. It takes a macro view of Scripture and redemptive history to fully grasp this idea. For example, consider the dietary laws described at length in the Books of Deuteronomy and Leviticus. At first glance, explanations about which animals are clean and which are unclean appear to have nothing at all to do with prophecy. They look more like a tedious menu of regulations designed to set God's people apart and test their devotion to Him.

But when you view the dietary rules in the larger context of redemptive history, you realize they have less to do with nutrition and more to do with God's eternal purpose. This is where the prophetic aspect of all Scripture—even the dietary laws—comes into view.

All Scripture is prophecy.

Do you remember the Acts 10 account of Peter's vision at Simon the tanner's house in Joppa? Peter was on the rooftop praying and became hungry. While lunch was being prepared, he fell into a trance. The backstory, of which Peter was not yet aware, was that God had sent an angel to speak to an Italian man of prayer named Cornelius. The angel told Cornelius to send for Peter and bring him back to Cornelius' home in Caesarea.

The timing of Peter's vision is significant; it occurred as Cornelius' messengers were about to invite Peter to accompany them. The vision was entirely prophetic:

> [Peter] *saw the sky opened up, and an object like a great sheet*
> *coming down, lowered by four corners to the ground, and there*
> *were in it all kinds of four-footed animals and crawling creatures*
> *of the earth and birds of the air. And a voice came to him, "Get*
> *up, Peter, kill and eat!" But Peter said, "By no means, Lord, for*
> *I have never eaten anything unholy and unclean." And again a*
> *voice came to him a second time, "What God has cleansed, no*
> *longer consider unholy"* (Acts 10:11-15).

God used the vision to demonstrate that Peter's continuing ties to the Law had become a hindrance to his ministry. To Peter, the idea of eating "unclean" creatures was revolting. He still ascribed to the dietary laws of Torah and would not have dreamed of eating such animals. Yet the voice said, *"Get up...kill and eat!"* When Peter resisted the voice explained that his dietary preferences were anachronistic and contrary to God's eternal purpose, saying, *"What God has cleansed, no longer consider unholy."*

Peter grappled with the heavenly admonition as Cornelius' team arrived. God knew that Peter would have second thoughts about obliging the Italian from Caesarea, so *"the Spirit said to him, '..."Get up, go downstairs, and accompany them without misgivings; for I have sent them Myself"'* (Acts 10:19-20). Peter's misgivings had been divinely set aside. The next day, he and the three men left Joppa.

There was nothing coincidental about the vision Peter received the day before his journey to Caesarea. It was sent by God to adjust Peter's doctrine and bring him into alignment with God's intent regarding the Gentiles (of whom Cornelius was one). Peter addressed the issue as soon as he arrived in Caesarea and revealed the connection between the vision and his visit:

> *You yourselves know how unlawful it is for a man who is a Jew*
> *to associate with a foreigner or to visit him; and yet God has*
> *shown me that I should not call any man unholy or unclean*
> (Acts 10:28).

Peter then shared the testimony of Jesus Christ. As he spoke, God moved on the people, and His eternal purpose was revealed:

*While Peter was still speaking...the Holy Spirit fell upon all
those who were listening to the message. And all the circumcised [Jewish] believers who had come with Peter were
amazed, because the gift of the Holy Spirit had been poured
out upon the Gentiles also. For they were hearing them speaking with tongues and exalting God. Then Peter answered,
"Surely no one can refuse the water for these to be baptized
who have received the Holy Spirit just as we did, can he?" And
he ordered them to be baptized in the name of Jesus Christ...*
(Acts 10:44-48).

Up till this point, the Church consisted almost entirely of Jews, even
though God's plan was to redeem all peoples! (See Mark 16:15.) The Church
had become exclusionary. God drew a parallel between the Church's condition and the exclusionary practices of the Law. By commanding Peter to see
all the creatures in his vision as being clean, God communicated His *inclu-
sionary* redemptive intent and inspired needed changes to the apostle's
ministry approach.

Can you see that the vision on Simon's rooftop had nothing to do
with food? The dietary laws themselves were prophetic. They were
intended for a larger purpose; now their role as prophetic metaphor was
evident. Remember that the Jews naturally divided the world into "clean"
and "unclean." Foods, practices, nations, tribes—all were judged by the
Law. The Jews distinguished clean from unclean peoples in part by what
they ate. Unclean foods and practices demonstrated the reality that some
nations were far from Him. Now, in the post-ascension paradigm, the
Way had been made to purify the unclean and bring them back to God.
As Paul would later write in Ephesians 2:19, the Gentiles were *"no longer
strangers and aliens."*

All Scripture is prophecy. Peter not only received a course correction
from Heaven; he also saw the prophetic fulfillment of dietary regulations in
the salvation of the Gentiles of Cornelius' household.

The Church's Jews-only mold had begun to break.

RELUCTANT OUTREACH

There is irony in Peter's reticence to reach the Gentiles: it stands in stark contrast to the prophecy in Joel 2:28 about God pouring out His *"Spirit on all mankind"*—a text Peter quoted on the Day of Pentecost! Later on, God used Saul, one of Christianity's foremost persecutors, to reach the Gentiles. Even Saul's persecuting ways helped spread the Gospel. As Christians fled his wrath, they carried the testimony from Jerusalem to Judea and Samaria!

Covenant Community From Testament to Testament

All Scripture is prophecy and all Scripture harmonizes, from Old Testament to New. This harmony confirms the divine inspiration and inerrancy of the Bible and highlights the threads that connect Old and New Covenant faith communities. Although the Church views the Old Covenant through the lens of the New, we neither discard nor disregard the Old, because God never deviates from His fixed principles. Jesus Himself said that He came not to abolish but to fulfill the Law and the Prophets (see Matt. 5:17).

The harmony of covenants is reflected in the parallel arrangements of their respective books. We are about to see a small blueprint of this harmony in the Book of Jeremiah. But first, let's discuss a little history. Remember that, in his day, the weeping prophet, Jeremiah, was harshly persecuted. His warnings of judgment fell on deaf ears and caused many to declare him a false seer. In their zeal to discredit Jeremiah, his detractors said, *"The law shall not perish from the priest, nor counsel from the wise, nor the word from the prophet"* (Jer. 18:18 NKJV).

In this sentence, Jeremiah's persecutors spoke the truth, although they had done so from wrong motives and a flawed assessment of the prophet, his ministry, and the times. They defended *a* truth at the expense of a man whose life was dedicated to *the* truth. Their cutting words touted God's view but rejected His servant and therefore, the God who sent him! (See Matthew 10:40.)

In his book *The Creative Word*,[1] Walter Brueggemann sees in Jeremiah 18:18 a map of the Old Testament that charts three sections: "the Torah, of the priest, the counsel of the wise, the word of the prophet."[2] We often refer to them as the Law, the Prophets, and the Wisdom Literature (or the Writings). These sections represent distinct modes of life and education[3] that have undergirded the covenant community since the Exodus. We will soon see how the New Testament parallels this progression, but first, let's take a brief tour of the Old.

Torah

The Torah is the first and preeminent portion of Old Covenant canon. From its five books (also called the Pentateuch or Law) flow the rest of Scripture. Torah tells us where we came from; it reveals both our human and community origins. Genesis describes the Creation, the life of Abraham, and the beginnings of the Hebrew nation. In Exodus, God delivers His people and establishes His Law. Leviticus teaches God's people how to approach Him in holiness. In Numbers they learn how to organize themselves spiritually, socially, and militarily. The fifth book, Deuteronomy, stresses the merits of covenant-keeping.

e·thos

"The distinguishing character, sentiment, moral nature, or guiding beliefs of a person, group, or institution..."[4]

The five books cover every aspect of life. Therefore, Brueggemann describes Torah as a "statement of community *ethos*."[5] Torah reveals the community's character and consensus in terms of beliefs and behaviors the community values as being nonnegotiable. From generation to generation (and to the extent that they uphold the ethos) these parameters ensure the integrity of the community against the whims of personal opinion and the world's shifting ways. Under the tutelage of Torah, the community takes precedence over the individual; the Law does not conform to people; instead, those who enter the community learn to see reality in the context of Torah.[6]

The Prophets

The second section of Old Testament canon includes the minor and major prophets, as well as the Book of Joshua and other historical books such as First and Second Samuel, First and Second Kings, etc.[7] Brueggeman includes the historical books because "they do not chronicle the affairs of persons and nations, but they trace the impingement of God's Word and purpose..."[8] within the context of history. In other words, these books document the community's determination to follow the proceeding and eternal Word of God.

pa·thos

1: an element in experience or in artistic representation evoking pity or compassion

2: an emotion of sympathetic pity[9]

The Prophets deal with "the *pathos* of God and of Israel..."[10] and reveal the tension between His promises and the state of the community at any given moment. Considering the gaps that are common between God's ideal and current reality, anguish and indignation are familiar expressions in prophetic books, according to Brueggemann.[11]

The ethos expressed by Torah and the pathos of the Prophets are intertwined. Theologian Abraham Joshua Heschel explains that *pathos* is a "concern for the world" and "the very ethos of God."[12] He describes this pathos as the "anxiety of God"[13] voiced by His prophets when the ethos is dishonored and the covenant is broken. The Prophets proclaim where the covenant community should be *and* where it is going.

lo·gos

A word which, uttered by the living voice, embodies a conception or idea; (Heb. 12:19)...of the moral precepts given by God in the O.T.: (Mark 7:13)...what is communicated by instruction...[14] The ancient Greek meaning of *logos* implies "meaning."[15]

Wisdom Literature

This is the section of Old Testament canon that Brueggemann refers to as "the Writings."[16] They correspond to Jeremiah 18:18's *"counsel of the wise,"* the most overt example of a wisdom book being the Book of Proverbs.[17] This mixed grouping includes all remaining Old Testament books. The Writings are not homogenous, yet they provide a sense of meaning and order to life and are therefore described as the *logos* of Old Testament canon.[18]

The Writings link past and future by shedding light on why we are here and how we are to conduct our earthly lives. They focus on experiential learning, the realization of potential, and the application of godly authority. From cultural and historical perspectives, this instruction was most often available in royal circles. Remember that, spiritually speaking, God sees His people as a kingdom of priests called to reign in life as a royal priesthood (see Exod. 19:6; Rom. 5:17; 1 Pet. 2:9).

In their totality, the Torah, the Prophets, and the Wisdom Literature reveal:

- Who we are,
- Where we came from,
- And where we are going.

New Covenant Parallel

The New Testament parallel to the progression in Jeremiah 18:18 (Torah, the Prophets, and Wisdom Literature) is seen in the Gospels, the Epistles, and the Book of Revelation.

The Gospels

The Gospels lay the groundwork for all else in the New Testament. As Torah did for the Old Covenant community, they mark the roots of the Church. First and foremost, the accounts document Jesus' earthly walk and set the stage for the emergence of the Church. Jesus' frequent references to Moses, Abraham, and other fathers in the faith reinforce the roots of the faith community. The genealogies presented in Matthew 1 and Luke 3 point to our origins as a people. The first chapter of John's Gospel takes us back to the Creation itself.

As with the Torah, the Gospels describe the laws of the Kingdom. This time, they are pronounced, not by the prophet Moses, but *the* Prophet, Jesus Christ. The Sermon on the Mount could be called the "Magna Carta" of the Kingdom. As a signature and comprehensive teaching, it defines the spiritual parameters of our community and maps our identity in the Messiah's own words.

The Book of Revelation

Although numerous prophecies are found in the Gospels and elsewhere (consider, among many other examples, John 2:19, in which Jesus said He would raise the Temple in three days) the Book of Revelation encapsulates God's prophetic intention in apocalyptic and concentrated form. In it Jesus addresses both the early and modern Church, both through His letters to the seven churches and through the entirety of the Revelation. In addition, the book explains where the Church is going in redemptive history, naming distinct events such as the Tribulation, Armageddon, and the millennial reign.

Revelation simultaneously stakes out our roots and current condition, and reminds us where we should be, spiritually speaking. Take, for example, Jesus' assessment of the church at Ephesus (and by extension, segments of today's Church). It reads like a report card, as all seven letters do. Jesus commends the church for her deeds, toil, and perseverance, as well as her diligence in testing those who call themselves apostles (see Rev. 2:2). This is Jesus' assessment of the church's condition. His evaluation of where the church should be is revealed in Revelation 2:4, where He warns: *"But I have this against you, that you have left your first love."* The Church should be focused on her first love, but is not.

In the larger sense, the Book of Revelation reveals the glorious future of the Church, but also articulates finer points as to where the Church will end up if His warnings go heeded: *"Therefore remember from where you have fallen, and repent and do the deeds you did at first; or else I am coming to you, and will remove your lampstand out of its place..."* (Rev. 2:5). Jesus' warnings testify that any church that deserts its first love and fails to correct itself will become irrelevant.

The Epistles

Finally, we have the New Testament "wisdom section": the Epistles. These books teach us how to behave in accordance with God's eternal purpose. They connect the dots between where we started and where we are going by providing theological and practical instruction. Paul's second epistle to Timothy is a good example:

> *Be strong in the grace that is in Christ Jesus. And the things which you have heard from me in the presence of many witnesses, these entrust to faithful men, who will be able to teach others also* (2 Timothy 2:1-2).

Paul mentioned the theological reality of grace; he also established a practical method for Timothy's handling of the revelation he received. Paul urged him to pass on what he learned to faithful believers who would, in turn, teach others. This is wisdom in New Testament form: it delineates the journey from our unsaved beginnings, to the transformative point of our salvation, and forward to the filling of all things (see Eph. 4:10) and the grooming of a Church without spot or wrinkle (see Eph. 5:27).

Torah	The Prophets	Wisdom Literature
The Gospels	The Book of Revelation	The Epistles

The Nexus of Old and New

The Old and New Covenant parallels are more than a curiosity. They are the context from which we can compare and contrast Old and New Covenant prophetic expression. Moses accurately stated that the Prophet, the Messiah, would be like him (see Deut. 18:15). Moses knew by the Spirit of God that he was part of the Old Covenant template; he was a prototype describing aspects of the New-Covenant prophet and apostle.

Just as the three New Testament divisions reflect the Old Testament template seen in Jeremiah 18:18, post-ascension prophets are best understood in comparison to Old Covenant types. Whether we are discussing Scripture in general or the prophetic in particular, this principle holds: the Old Covenant is but a shadow; the New reveals the substance or *fulfillment.* Hebrews 10:1 says, *"The Law...has only a shadow of the good things to come and not the very form of things, can never by the same sacrifices year by year... make perfect those who draw near."*

Just as the Law found its fulfillment in Jesus Christ, the Old Testament prophets find their fulfillment in members of His Body.

Shadow and Fulfillment

The fullness of God's thought revealed in the New Covenant is in perfect harmony with the Old. The connection is indelible, but so is the contrast. Colossians 2:16-17 fine-tunes the post-ascension perspective of the two covenants:

> *No one is to act as your judge in regard to food or drink or in respect to a festival or a new moon or a Sabbath day* [the Law]—*things which are a mere **shadow** of what is to come; but the **substance** belongs to Christ.*

The qualities of shadow help us to explain the harmony of the covenants. Shadow reveals shape but only in outline form. The full light is lacking or obscured; therefore detail and color are muted. Spiritually speaking, the full light is not released until the fullness of time; yet the existence of shadow (which can only form in the presence of light) implies light that has already come. In the case of the covenants, the shadow of the Old spoke from the beginning of the already existing substance of the New. In other words, God declared the end from the beginning:

> *Remember the former things long past, for I am God, and there is no other; I am God, and there is no one like Me, declaring the end from the beginning and from ancient times things which have not been done, saying, "My purpose will be established, and I will accomplish all My good pleasure"* (Isaiah 46:9-10).

So the shadow (the Old Covenant) implied that the substance (the New Covenant) existed before it was known by man. This is not a human way of seeing history; yet it is God's way. Remember His words to Adam and Eve in The Garden: *"And I will put enmity between you and the woman, and between your seed and her seed; He shall bruise you on the head, and you shall bruise Him on the heel"* (Gen. 3:15). His redemptive plan was in place even before the Law was given!

Shadows of the Prophetic and Apostolic

In the Book of Exodus, the prophetic and apostolic are revealed in shadow form by two of Moses' contemporaries. When the Tabernacle was to be built, Moses said, *"See, the Lord has called by name Bezalel...of the tribe of Judah...[and] filled him with the Spirit of God, in wisdom, in understanding and in knowledge and in all craftsmanship"* (Exod. 35:30-31).

Bezalel would use his God-given gifts and talents in the building of the structure and in teaching. He would work with Oholiab, a man similarly gifted and used of God (see Exod. 35:34-35). Together they would build the Tabernacle and its furnishings, arranging them as God ordained. Their collaborative work created *the* space in which God desired His people to worship Him.

Building and teaching are intrinsic qualities of apostles and prophets: The apostle "builds" the covenant community upon sound doctrine. The prophet inspects the building and its materials, compares them to the divine blueprint, provides understanding, and ensures the forward movement of the community in the direction of the fullness of Christ.

The names of these prophetic and apostolic forerunners illuminate God's intent. *Bezalel* means "in the shadow of God."[19] *Oholiab* means "tent of his father."[20] In combination, they present in shadow form the New Testament model which involves the continual building of the household of God.

Gift Preview

Any discussion of the prophetic must include an understanding of the prophet. We will distinguish later between the more general prophetic giftings and the office of the prophet. First, let's briefly consider a key verse underpinning the distinction: *"When He ascended on high, He led captive a host of captives, and **He gave gifts to men"** (Eph. 4:8).

The passage goes on to describe the gifts as apostles, prophets, evangelists, pastors, and teachers. These are referred to as the *fivefold ministry* or *ascension gifts*. (Please note that some view the pastor-teacher as a single gift. For our purposes, we will name them separately.) Ephesians 4 is not the sole mention of spiritual gifts; Romans 12 and First Corinthians 12 also list gifts. Those mentioned in Ephesians 4, however, are distinguished by the use of the Greek word *doma*, which is not applied to the other groupings. According to *Vine's Expository Dictionary of New Testament Words*, *doma* "lends greater stress to the concrete character of the 'gift'" and is "akin to [the Greek word] *demo*, 'to build, and denotes a housetop."[21]

We will explore the *doma* gifts in Chapters 3 and 4 and elsewhere. For now, suffice to say that *doma* gifts are not just gifts *in* people. In the case of the office of prophet, for example, the prophet *is* the gift. The same is true of the offices of the apostle, evangelist, pastor, and teacher. They don't just have gifts; they are gifts. Although the doma (or ascension or fivefold ministry) gifts move in the spiritual gifts listed in Romans and First Corinthians, the doma gift is distinctive in function and development.

For example, many in the Body of Christ have prophetic tendencies and have ministered in that realm; yet not all are prophets. The prophetic office encompasses more than prophetic leanings. We will soon see how God creates and prepares His Ephesians 4:8 gifts—His *doma*—for service. But first, we will talk about God's eternal purpose.

Pinpoint the Prophetic

1. How does our discussion of the fuller meaning of the dietary laws impact your personal understanding of the statement that "all Scripture is prophecy"? What other examples illustrate this point?

2. How does the harmony of Old and New Covenants deepen your appreciation of the Old? How does it better equip you to discuss the inspiration and inerrancy of the Bible with skeptics?

3. Consider our discussion of shadow and substance. What questions did our discussion resolve for you? What points would you add?

4. Select a Bible character not named in this chapter, and study the meaning of his or her name (using any combination of concordances, lexicons, commentaries, etc.). How does the prophetic aspect of the character and story become clearer as a result of your research?

5. Consider our preliminary discussion of the gifts discussed in Ephesians 4. What new questions does it raise? Write them down and consider them as you read Chapters 3 and 4.

Chapter 2

God's Eternal Purpose

*...I am God, and there is no one like Me, declaring
the end from the beginning and from ancient times
things which have not been done, saying, "My
purpose will be established, and I will accomplish
all My good pleasure"* (ISAIAH 46:9-10).

THE ABOVE PASSAGE FROM ISAIAH ESTABLISHES A BROAD UNDER-
standing of God and His eternal purpose: God is entirely purposeful. He
declares and sees His desire completed before it is manifested before human
eyes. He spans all of time, all the time. His purpose is therefore eternal in
nature. Ultimately, His purpose *will* be fulfilled.

Our view of time is inadequate to understand eternity. We hear His
promises; we await their appearance in the period we call *the future*. Yet, we
know He declared them *"from the beginning"*—and we know that what He
declares is as good as done. What God asserts is made manifest in His timing and according to His *"good pleasure,"* which Gesenius' Lexicon defines
as that which delights Him, reflects His desire and will, is precious to Him,
and is His divine pursuit.[1]

You'll remember from our discussion of shadow and substance that the
existence of shadow implies the presence of light. God reveals His plan for

the future by casting the shadow of its prior and current existence. What God revealed in shadow to the pre-ascension faith community was only a hint of what was to come, but it was a strong hint—a picture not fully colored in, yet bearing witness that what was "to come" already existed in the eternity of God.

When Moses implored God, *"I pray You, show me Your glory!"* (Exod. 33:18), God agreed, saying, *"I will put you in the cleft of the rock and cover you with My hand until I have passed by. Then I will take My hand away and you shall see My back, but My face shall not be seen"* (Exod. 33:22-23). He would reveal Himself, but only partially. Moses would not be privy to all that was ahead. His place in the unfolding of redemptive history did not allow him to see the entire revelation. Instead, God revealed to Moses the shadow of the Son of God, *"the Lamb slain from the foundation of the world"* (Rev. 13:8 KJV).

God's ultimate and eternal purpose—all He ordained to be accomplished through His Son in the fullness of time—had been moving through time *"from the foundation of the world."* The light of God had shone upon the Son already; it was the light that allowed Moses to see Him in shadow. From God's eternal perspective, the Lamb of God had already been slain.

Now, the Lamb of God has been slain before the eyes of humankind. Therefore, we have *"a better covenant...enacted on better promises"* (Heb. 8:6). Even so, *"we know in part, and we prophesy in part"* (1 Cor. 13:9). Even now, with the anointing of the indwelling Holy Spirit that has been released to God's people under the New Covenant, only the Holy Spirit knows the full details of God's eternal plan and purpose.

God Is Intentional

God is the ultimate Leader; His direction is clear, and He communicates it with precision. He reveals enough of the inner workings of His Kingdom for us to be effective participants. Through Isaiah, God provided a clear sense of how He sets His plan and purpose in motion:

> So shall My word be which goes forth from My mouth; it shall not return to Me empty, without accomplishing what I desire, and without succeeding in the matter for which I sent it (Isaiah 55:11).

Although God is complex, He is not ambiguous. The above verse proclaims that He says what He means and means what He says. So unfettered is His intentionality that when He speaks, His eternal purpose is both expressed and fulfilled in the release of His words. God is unswervingly intentional; He never deviates from His eternal purpose.

in·tent

1. something that is intended; purpose; design; intention...

2. the act or fact of intending, as to do something...

3. ...the state of a person's mind that directs his or her actions toward a specific object.

4. meaning or significance.[2]

Random House defines *intent* as something more than a thought scribbled on a to-do list. Intent is born of purpose that inspires design. Sincere intent leads to action; it propels us in the direction of a specific object or goal. Intent is substantive; its weightiness issues from the meaning and significance of the "intender's" desired result.

God's intent is one with His eternal purpose and always leads to the accomplishment of His *"good pleasure"* (Isa. 46:10). Like everything God is and does, His intent is complete, lacking nothing that is needed to bring His plan to fruition. Because He is changeless, His intent does not waver or wane. It functions continually in the face of all circumstances and produces a continuum of results.

God is unswervingly intentional; He never deviates from His eternal purpose.

Our vision is sometimes muddied when adversity or insecurity clouds our view of life's big picture. Not so with God; He fully—without hesitation, worry, or second-guessing—expects to see His intent unfold. Everything

God says, does, and thinks is inherently prophetic; His intent is like living seed that awaits germination.

God's Intent Unfolds in the Wilderness

If God's intent is immutable, can it be thwarted? Keep this question in mind as we explore a season in the earthly walk of Jesus that appeared to muddle God's eternal purpose but was in fact divinely appointed.

During His 40-day fast in the wilderness, when Jesus was tempted by satan to turn stones into bread, He responded to the demonic invitation to satisfy His hunger with these powerful words: *"It is written, 'Man shall not live on bread alone, but on every word that proceeds out of the mouth of God'"* (Matt. 4:4). According to Adam Clarke's Commentary, *"but on every word"* means:

> Not only a word spoken, but also thing, purpose, appointment, etc. Our Lord's meaning seems to be this: God purposes the welfare of his creatures—all his appointments are calculated to promote this end. Some of them may appear to man to have a contrary tendency; but even fasting itself, when used in consequence of a divine injunction, becomes a mean [sic] of supporting that life which it seems naturally calculated to impair or destroy.[3]

Jesus' encounter with satan was the unfolding of God's purpose; after all, He *"was led up by the Spirit into the wilderness to be tempted by the devil"* (Matt. 4:1). It was no doubt a grueling experience for a man who'd foregone food *and* water for 40 days. Nevertheless, it was literally a divine appointment "calculated to promote"[4] "the welfare of his creatures"[5] by further positioning Jesus and the devil for their ultimate encounter at Calvary.

Notice that Jesus compared the words proceeding from God's mouth to bread. God's Word both carries and nourishes His eternal purpose. His Word brings nourishment wherever it is released and embraced—in trials, in decision-making, in the fulfillment of destiny. Jesus cleaved to God's Word and quoted it, thereby refuting and disposing of every temptation satan conjured. Jesus' adherence to God's truth (and, therefore, His intent and eternal purpose) ensured the unfolding of God's plan for the Christ.

Jesus' steadfast cooperation with God's intent should inform our lives. He has issued a proceeding word over each of us; it is a word soaked in God's eternal purpose. If embraced, it will nourish and empower us to stand firm in God's plan, even in the wilderness.

God's Intent and Our Destiny

Which brings us back to our question: Can God's intent be thwarted? The answer is twofold. God's ultimate intent to fill all things in Christ (see Eph. 4:10) cannot be undone. Father, Son, and Holy Spirit are in one accord; the intent expressed in Paul's letter to the Ephesians will be accomplished.

God's intent for us as individuals, or for our respective churches and families, requires our cooperation. His intent can be frustrated, hindered, and even sabotaged when our intentionality wavers. Because we are free moral agents who can choose to disobey or disregard God's intent, the fullness of His ultimate will for each of us can only be accomplished with our agreement.

Back in my Bible school days, I heard a statement that is common in the Christian lexicon and widely accepted. It is a seemingly innocuous remark that is passively received as truth and thoughtlessly passed from generation to generation. Unless it is subjected to the rigors of critical thinking, the idea holds fast despite its fallacy. The gist is this: *If you do not fulfill your destiny, God will give it to someone else to fulfill.*

It sounds logical: If God's eternal plan and purpose to fill all things in Christ cannot be denied, then whatever He planned to accomplish through our lives must be fulfilled to the letter. Therefore, if we resist His leading, He will find another vessel to take up our work. The Lord of glory will shout, "Next!" and issue our marching orders to someone else.

This sounds like common sense, but God's ways are uncommon. The premise assumes that our individual destinies are interchangeable. *This is not so.* God creates no cookie-cutter lives. You and I are one-of-a-kind, unrepeatable works of His craftsmanship. Each of our destinies is entirely unique in shape, scope, and "flavor." Your destiny is custom-fitted to your identity. As long as you choose to disregard or discard your destiny, whether through ignorance of your identity or outright rebellion, your destiny will remain unfulfilled. God will not assign your neighbor to pinch-hit for you, because your neighbor's destiny is also one-of-a-kind.

Your destiny cannot be retrofitted for download into someone else's life. What happens, then, to God's eternal plan? Will it be accomplished? Yes, it will. Perhaps the need you would have met through the use of your unique gifts and abilities will be met in another way and in different timing by someone else. It may be that those to whom you were called are none the wiser to what might have been. The finer point is this: the totality of your destiny with all of its myriad implications can be fulfilled by just one person—*you*.

Q: Are spirituality and critical thinking compatible?

A: Critical thinking is an important aspect of spirituality. Although faith means believing in things that supersede the intellect or cannot be proven through the limits of scientific method, it does not demand that we suspend our intellect. We should always engage our critical-thinking skills, but resist putting God in boxes of our choosing. *"For as the heavens are higher than the earth, so are My ways higher than your ways, and My thoughts than your thoughts"* (Isa. 55:9).

God's Intent and the Fullness of Christ

Can you see the importance of our becoming as intentional about God's eternal purpose as He is? It is the only way we as individuals and as a Body can experience the complete unfolding of His glorious plan. And isn't that what we pray for day after day, year after year—to please Him and to live meaningful, productive, and rewarding lives?

Our prayers are fully answered and our lives fully flourish only when we align ourselves with God's intent. In a general sense, His intent is expressed in His Word. As we renew our minds (see Rom. 12:1-2) and embrace His general will, He begins to reveal successive aspects of His specific will for each of us. Even as He unfurls these finer points, we realize that knowing His will is only part of the equation. Committing to it is another. That is why we must ask the Holy Spirit to impress upon us the preeminence of God's intent to fill all things in Christ. To the extent that we become as intentional as He is we can participate in His plan to bring many sons to glory! (See Ephesians 4:10 and Hebrews 2:10.)

How can we be sure God's eternal purpose has not yet been fulfilled? For one thing, Jesus has not yet returned. Had the condition of the Church reflected the fullness of God's intent for her, the Second Coming would be a fact of history. Instead, He is waiting *"until we all attain to the unity of the faith, and of the knowledge of the Son of God, to a mature man, to the measure of the stature which belongs to the fullness of Christ"* (Eph. 4:13).

The fullness Paul depicts in Ephesians 4 is expressed by two forms of the same Greek root: the verb, *pleroo,* translated "fill" in verse 10 and the noun, *pleroma,* translated "fullness" in verse 13. Both forms describe a state or condition that is "replete" or "complete"[6]—a condition without flaw, lack, or discrepancy. God's glorious intent for the world and His Church is perfect!

re·plete

1. abundantly supplied or provided; filled[7]

com·plete

1. having all parts or elements; lacking nothing; whole; entire; full...

2. finished; ended; concluded...

3. having all the required or customary characteristics, skills, or the like; consummate; perfect in kind or quality...

4. thorough; entire; total; undivided, uncompromised, or unmodified...[8]

Clearly, we have not yet "arrived." In fact, we often contradict God's intent. At the very least, the Church contradicts the fullness of His intent. The world overtly resists Christ, as two minutes of television programming will reveal. Those living apart from Christ accept myriad substitutes to assuage the emptiness they feel. Many have convinced themselves and others that they don't need a Savior. They have accepted the worldly view that looking to the Savior is nothing more than a crutch for weak-minded, ignorant, or ungifted souls.

Others simply fail to recognize who Jesus is. With each generation's adoption of a Christ-less worldview, our fallen planet sinks deeper into darkness. In this epoch of history, darkness seems to increase exponentially, day by day.

Meanwhile, the Church continues to inch forward, all too often taking two steps forward and one back, like a man in a three-legged race. Whether our shortfalls result from the leaven of tradition, legalism, passivity, the denial of spiritual gifts, or the belief that those in the pews are called to be spectators to the work of the ministry, the fact remains that God never intended for us to take any steps backward. When we fully cooperate with His intent, the only direction is forward.

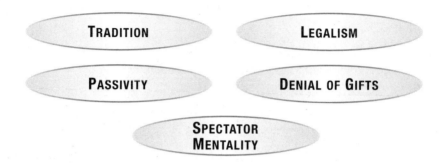

HINDRANCES TO THE FULLNESS OF CHRIST

TRADITION

LEGALISM

PASSIVITY

DENIAL OF GIFTS

SPECTATOR MENTALITY

Principles and Eternal Purpose

Just as the Church rests upon the foundation of apostles and prophets, with Jesus Christ as her Chief Cornerstone, God's eternal purpose rests on fixed principles, some of which we sampled in regard to the Church's identity. The following list is not exhaustive but provides a broader view, beginning at the top, so to speak.

Christ is seated at the Father's right hand. Paul exhorted the church at Colossae, articulating what is perhaps the greatest principle of the Church: *"If then you have been raised up with Christ, keep seeking the things above, where Christ is, seated at the right hand of God"* (Col. 3:1). Jesus' assumption of this heavenly position of authority (and our having been "raised up with [Him]") must be grasped for the Church and her genuine apostolic and prophetic leaders to grow and fulfill their callings within the larger picture of His eternal purpose.

The Church is built on the foundation of apostles and prophets, with Jesus as the Chief Cornerstone (see Eph. 2:20). Jesus is the Head of the Church, the One through whom all members of the Body are connected in purpose, function, and placement. Psalms 118:22 (believed by many to be the writing of David) prophesied: *"The stone which the builders rejected has become the chief cornerstone"* (NKJV). The Hebrew here refers to the "head stone of the corner,"[9] with the word *corner* meaning a "bulwark, chief, corner, stay, tower."[10]

Merriam-Webster defines *bulwark* as "a solid wall-like structure raised for defense...a strong support or protection"[11] and defines *tower* as a structure that is "...high relative to its surroundings...one that provides support or protection."[12] While Jesus is the Head of His Church, He is the ultimate *Servant*-Leader who supports and protects His people.

Jesus testified to His fulfillment of Psalm 118:22 before the chief priests and Pharisees when He asked this pointed question: *"Have you never read in the Scriptures: 'The stone which the builders rejected has become the chief cornerstone. This was the Lord's doing, and it is marvelous in our eyes'?"* (Matt. 21:42 NKJV). Though the religious leaders of the day knew the prophecy of the Chief Cornerstone and claimed to understand God's eternal purpose, they failed to recognize their Messiah when He appeared in plain sight.

The only message is Christ, the Chief Cornerstone of God's building. Under the inspiration of the Holy Spirit, Luke wrote, *"There is salvation in no one else; for there is no other name under heaven that has been given among men, by which we must be saved"* (Acts 4:12). Jesus said, *"I am the way, and the truth, and the life; no one comes to the Father, but through Me"* (John 14:6).

Without Jesus, there is no Church. He is our Head, and we are His Body; therefore our only message is Christ. True apostles and prophets are consumed with talking about Him. Any message that purports to move beyond the message of Christ and His Church is suspect. Any message that fails to mention Him and revolve around Him is not *of* Him! The testimony of Jesus Christ is *the* message of His Church.

Everything we learn must be seen through the lens of Christ, His cross, and His resurrection. When we study the Old Testament, we do so with the understanding of shadow and substance, the former covenant and the better covenant, respectively (see Heb. 7:22; 8:6). We hold up the words of the prophets and other Old Testament servants of the Light that is Christ, the One who fulfilled their covenant.

Even our callings are seen through the filter of His finished work. His example forms the context in which we serve Him and others. We do not center our efforts or achievements on self. Instead, we learn who He is, and by His grace, we imitate Him (see Eph. 5:1). For the follower of Christ, all the *"issues of life"* (Prov. 4:23 NKJV) must be seen through the reality of redemption or they will be misunderstood. This includes all personal issues and even matters of politics, finance, and culture. All thoughts and actions must be drawn through the sieve of God's eternal purpose as revealed in Jesus Christ.

With the Chief Cornerstone in mind, the Church will be continually built up. Although the pre-ascension faith community saw the Messiah in their future, the post-ascension message could not be preached until the Redeemer had come. Now that He has passed from death to life, ascended to the Father, taken His seat at the Father's right hand, and poured out His Spirit upon us, *everything* in our lives rests upon His finished work—and everything we say should, too.

The message of Christ is the message of grace. The New Covenant message is centered on Christ and therefore, on grace. Remember His invitation:

> *Are you tired? Worn out? Burned out on religion? Come to Me. Get away with Me and you'll recover your life. I'll show you how to take a real rest. Walk with Me and work with Me—watch how I do it. Learn the unforced rhythms of grace. **I won't lay anything heavy or ill-fitting on you. Keep company with Me and you'll learn to live freely and lightly*** (Matthew 11:28-30 MSG).

The New Covenant has not been wrought in the blood of animals or the blood, sweat, and tears of humankind. It was been rendered in Christ's blood only. Because He did all this *for* us, our only required action is to receive it. That is grace: we cannot enter into it through our efforts; it is received as a gift, and it causes us to become more Christlike with each passing day.

Although grace calls us out from under the Law, it does not discredit the Law. Galatians 3:24-28 explains the purpose of the former covenant:

> *The Law has become our tutor to lead us to Christ, that we may be justified by faith. But now that faith has come, we are no*

longer under a tutor. For you are all sons of God through faith in Christ Jesus. For all of you who were baptized into Christ have clothed yourselves with Christ. There is neither Jew nor Greek, there is neither slave nor free man, there is neither male nor female; for you are all one in Christ Jesus.

Those who preach the message of Christ must proclaim the *New* Covenant of grace. It is a pillar of God's eternal purpose!

The message and the messenger are one. In coming chapters, we will see just how the post-ascension message and messenger are one. Because the prophet *is* the message, any prophet God intends to raise up in the Body of Christ must first go through a process of becoming the message (specifically, the message of grace).

We are no longer aliens to the Kingdom. Galatians 3:28 says that we are *"all one in Christ Jesus"* regardless of religious upbringing, ethnicity, gender, or stature in the community. Colossians 1:13 says, *"He delivered us from the domain of darkness, and transferred us to the kingdom of His beloved Son...."* Therefore, we *"are no longer strangers and aliens, but...fellow citizens with the saints, and are of God's household..."* (Eph. 2:19).

In his letter to the Ephesians, Paul carefully described God's open invitation to Kingdom citizenship. The early Church originally consisted primarily of Jews, who were the first to hear the Gospel (see Rom. 1:16). Paul knew that God did not intend the Church to be a "Jewish-only" club (see Acts 9:15; 13:47). Paul was called to reach the Gentiles, because *"God so loved **the world"*** (John 3:16 NKJV).

As an elite Hebrew scholar, Paul recognized that the distinction between Jews and Gentiles had served its purpose under the Old Covenant. Under the New Covenant, such exclusions would be anathema. We must always honor the Jewish people and pray for Israel (see Rom. 8:16 and Ps. 122:6). We are not called, however, to exalt any nation or race, theologically speaking, above any other in the Body of Christ. There are no second-class citizens in the Church. Instead, *"Gentiles are fellow heirs* [with the Jews] *and fellow members of the body, and fellow partakers of the promise in Christ Jesus through the gospel"* (Eph. 3:6).

The Culmination of History

At the heart of the Father's infallible, immutable intent is the filling of all things in Christ—the culmination of history planned before the foundation of the world. The Lord's cry to all people is the same as it was to the Jews 2,000 years ago: *"How often I wanted to gather your children together, the way a hen gathers her chicks under her wings, and you were unwilling"* (Matt. 23:37).

Jesus' words should arrest the attention of the Church; they should remind us how easily and unexpectedly we can stray from God's eternal purpose. Whether we are seasoned saints or brand-new believers, we must always ask the Holy Spirit to reveal where we stand in relation to Christ filling all things in our lives. He will help us to distinguish between the dead works of dogma and the living riches of relationship with our Savior.

The Church and everyone in it are on a journey reflective of His fixed principles and the times in which we live. Our current season is marked by acceleration. Both the external changes in our world and our internal maturation in Christ seem to be operating with increased velocity. Our focus is also shifting: in this season, we are less concerned with where the Father has brought us *from* and more absorbed with where He is taking us *to*. We don't peer from the present toward the past; instead we gaze into present and future.

The future is moving from shadow to substance according to the eternal purpose of the Most High God.

Pinpoint the Prophetic

1. How does our human view of past, present, and future differ from God's eternal view? Give an example of where and/or how the two viewpoints collide.

2. Describe two qualities of God's intentionality. Using these as your measuring stick, explain how human intentionality sometimes falls short.

3. Have you uncovered any areas in which God's intent for your destiny has been hindered? Explain.

4. Describe how Jesus' role as the Chief Cornerstone is reflected in the conduct of your life. What strength does the Chief Cornerstone supply? What aspects of your life might better reflect His role?

5. What aspects of your life best reflect the message of Christ? Describe areas in which any discrepancy has become evident to you.

Chapter 3

The Ascension Gifts—Part I

The gifts which Jesus Christ distributes to man he has received in man, in and by virtue of his incarnation; and it is in...his being made man that...The Lord God dwells among them.... This view...is consistent with the whole economy of grace....[1] —Adam Clarke's Commentary

THE HUMAN IMAGINATION IS STRETCHED BY WHAT ADAM CLARKE called God's "economy of grace." Because God loved (and still loves) fallen humankind, the Savior gave all that was needed to restore us. He spared nothing, not even His blood. So after making the ultimate sacrifice, did the Savior require gifts from those whose souls were saved?

No, He ascended and gave even more; He gave the ascension gifts, namely the apostle, prophet, evangelist, pastor, and teacher. The giving of these gifts had been foretold in the psalms. In his letter to the Ephesians, Paul tied the psalmist's prophecy to the Church age.

Adam Clarke's commentary on Ephesians 4:8 compares the passages:

Thou hast ascended on high, Thou hast led captivity captive; **Thou hast received gifts for men,** *yea, for the rebellious also, that the Lord God may dwell among them* (Psalm 68:18 KJV).

> *Therefore it says, "When He ascended on high, He led captive a host of captives, and **He gave gifts to men.**" (Now this expression, "He ascended," what does it mean except that He also had descended into the lower parts of the earth? He who descended is Himself also He who ascended far above all the heavens, that He might fill all things.) And He gave some as **apostles, and some as prophets, and some as evangelists, and some as pastors and teachers,** for the equipping of the saints for the work of service, to the building up of the body of Christ; until we all attain to the unity of the faith, and of the knowledge of the Son of God, to a mature man, to the measure of the stature which belongs to the fullness of Christ* (Ephesians 4:8-13).

In Psalm 68, David wrote that the Lord *"received gifts for men."* Paul's letter explained that *"He gave gifts to men."* The differences in verbiage suggest contradiction; but Adam Clarke disagrees. He explains that David's words imply the receiving of gifts *for man* or *in man.*[2] Further word study supports Clarke's position and reveals the implication of "taking [gifts] to or for a person"[3] or infolding or placing gifts.[4]

Spiritual gifts were not new; they were evident in the lives of Old Covenant figures including Moses and the major and minor prophets. As stunning as their gifts were, they were a shadow of what was ahead. Only *after* Jesus *"ascended on high, [and] led captive a host of captives"* (Eph. 4:8) would the fullness of the gifts' operation and authority be possible.

Pentecost and God's Prophetic Instrument

The first appearance of the ascension gifts in their full bloom occurred on a momentous day in the Upper Room—the Day of Pentecost:

> *When the day of Pentecost had come, they were all together in one place. And suddenly there came from heaven a noise like a violent rushing wind, and it filled the whole house where they were sitting. And there appeared to them tongues as of fire distributing themselves, and they rested on each one of them.*

And they were all filled with the Holy Spirit and began to speak with other tongues, as the Spirit was giving them utterance (Acts 2:1-4).

This was the God-appointed day on which the Holy Spirit filled the apostles and others to overflowing. Although Jesus had appointed His 12 original apostles during His earthly ministry, it was only after Pentecost that they truly understood their commissioning and realized the level of effectiveness for which they had been set apart. At the crux of their newfound efficacy was the Holy Spirit. In Acts 1:5, Jesus reminded them of what John the Baptist had prophesied three years earlier: the second baptism. At the height of his ministry John declared: *"I baptize you with water for repentance, but...He will baptize you with the Holy Spirit and fire"* (Matt. 3:11).

After Jesus' resurrection and before He ascended to Heaven, He gave the apostles further instruction regarding the Holy Spirit, saying, *"you shall receive power when the Holy Spirit has come upon you; and you shall be My witnesses both in Jerusalem, and in all Judea and Samaria, and even to the remotest part of the earth"* (Acts 1:8). Jesus had indicated before Calvary that this event would occur in Jerusalem when He told them to *"tarry...until ye be endued with power from on high"* (Luke 24:49 KJV).

When the promised day came, 120 followers of Christ gathered in the Upper Room and declared the wonderful works of God in languages unknown to them but miraculously recognized by others. The Church was birthed in earnest and became God's prophetic instrument in the earth.

On the Day of Pentecost, the Church was birthed in earnest and became God's prophetic instrument in the earth.

Peter, the once-fearful apostle who denied Jesus not once but three times (see Luke 22), now began to preach the Gospel boldly and with power. For the sake of the Jews who had not yet believed, he wasted no time connecting the dots between Moses and Jesus Christ. Peter quoted Moses' own words before those gathered at the portico of Solomon:

> *Moses said, "The Lord God shall raise up for you a prophet like*
> *me from your brethren; to Him you shall give heed in everything*
> *He says to you. And it shall be that every soul that does not heed*
> *that prophet shall be utterly destroyed from among the people"*
> (Acts 3:22-23).

Peter challenged those who had rejected the Chief Cornerstone. He called them to repent, return to God, and receive the refreshing of the Holy Spirit (see Acts 3:19) so that they could take their places in the Body of Christ and do the work of the Church. He reminded them of *"the things which God announced beforehand by the mouth of all the prophets, that His Christ would suffer"* and made clear that what God had promised had now occurred in plain sight (see Acts 3:18).

The prophets Peter referenced for the sake of the Jews were not the new breed of ascension prophets but those beginning with Abraham and ending with John the Baptist. Their example laid the groundwork for the ascension gifts, but their ministry model differed from those who would prophesy after Christ. Because they were the product of a *new* covenant, the ascension gifts would operate under new principles. Instead of focusing on the coming Messiah, the gifts would now reflect the reality that Jesus Christ was seated at the Father's right hand!

> ### FIVE: THE NUMBER OF GRACE
>
> The *fivefold ministry* is comprised of five distinct ascension
> gifts (called *doma* in the Greek): apostle, prophet, evangelist,
> pastor, and teacher. In God's design, these gifts come by way
> of grace and attest to grace by their number.

Doma Versus Charismata

The ascension gifts are not the only New Covenant gifts found in Scripture. However, they are the ones mentioned when Ephesians 4:8 declares that Jesus *"ascended on high...led captive a host of captives, and...gave gifts to men"* (Eph. 4:8). In Chapter 1, we learned the significance of the Greek word *doma,* which is translated "gifts" in this verse. The word implies a gift of "concrete character"[5] and is not used elsewhere in Scripture. We learned that *doma* is "akin to *demo,* 'to build....'"[6]

Remember, the doma is not a gift carried by a person; instead, it *is* the person. This applies to all five gifts listed in Ephesians 4:11. *Doma* are distinct from the charismata described in Romans 12 and First Corinthians 12:

> *Since we have gifts that differ according to the grace given to us, let each exercise them accordingly: if* **prophecy,** *according to the proportion of his faith; if* **service,** *in his serving; or he who teaches, in his* **teaching;** *or he who exhorts, in his* **exhortation;** **he who gives,** *with liberality;* **he who leads,** *with diligence; he who shows* **mercy,** *with cheerfulness* (Romans 12:6-8).

> *To one is given the* **word of wisdom** *through the Spirit, and to another the* **word of knowledge** *according to the same Spirit; to another* **faith** *by the same Spirit, and to another* **gifts of healing** *by the one Spirit, and to another* **the effecting of miracles,** *and to another* **prophecy,** *and to another the* **distinguishing of spirits,** *to another various kinds of* **tongues,** *and to another* **the interpretation of tongues.** *But one and the same Spirit works all these things, distributing to each one individually just as He wills* (1 Corinthians 12:8-11).

This is not a book about the wide range of gifts found in the Body of Christ. The point here is to distinguish the doma gifts from other gifts. The charismata listed in the above passages from Romans and First Corinthians are grace endowments that operate through individuals, some of whom have strong tendencies in certain areas or operate in one or more gifts spontaneously or even randomly. For example, a believer might operate in the gift of prophecy (see Rom. 12:6; 1 Cor. 12:10) or be used at a particular moment to bring forth a word of wisdom or word of knowledge (see 1 Cor. 12:8). While these manifestations are essential and impactful, they do not establish the individual as a prophet. A prophet is not *endowed* with a gift; a prophet *is the gift.*

These prophetic endowments are designed to provide edification, comfort, and consolation. In other words, they build up, stir up, and lift up the believer and the Body. They are motivational in nature and inspire progress. Gifts, and especially the charismata, are never meant to beat up the sinner or the saint. For this reason, shepherds who encourage their sheep to flow in the gifts of the Spirit routinely counsel them against bringing prophetic messages that fail to edify, exhort, or console (see 1 Cor. 14:3).

The doma prophet is used by God to do all this and more, as we will see in coming chapters. As we learned earlier, the prophet ensures the forward movement of the Church by inspecting the "building" and comparing the structure and materials to the divine blueprint. The office of prophet is what we call a governmental gift; in other words, the prophet helps settle the Church in her foundation while confirming, establishing, and perfecting her. The prophet flags issues for the sake of the Body's well-being. Always, the prophet works alongside the apostle, who is God's appointed builder.

Q: What cautions should be applied to prophecy over the nations?

A: Prophets and prophecy must be held to account and judged by church elders. Prophesying to nations or national leaders is particularly tricky. In my experience and belief, this level of prophetic ministry should be delivered by seasoned ministers who are called to the office of the prophet and who have a known track record—in other words, there should be evidence that what they have prophesied to nations has come to pass. As far as prophesying judgment on nations or national leaders, this is almost exclusively outside the boundaries of prophetic function and almost always proves to be inaccurate.

Both doma and charismata are to be valued in the context of God's eternal purpose. Gifts are not curiosities. Seminars and schools that teach about prophetic gifts do well to proceed with caution, respecting the distinctions between doma and charismata and bringing clarification rather than confusion to the prophetic. Inviting well-intentioned or even misguided believers to attend classes and receive diplomas that confer the title of *prophet* is misleading at best. *Being* a prophet involves much more than the knowledge of how to prophesy.

The Doma Temperament

The doma is pre-built by God with a certain temperament or genius that is apparent to others. When you are in the company of a genuine evangelist, you know it. Evangelists' conversation, interaction—their *everything*—is centered on souls. The same is true for all doma gifts. They operate at a level of knowing and intelligence that exceeds those who were not formed to *be* the gift. That is not to say, for example, that apostles (who operate in the specific intelligence required by builders) are smarter than everyone else. It is to say that apostles exceed all others in the realm of apostolic intelligence.

The doma intelligence is recognized by others. Joshua recognized the rare attributes of his mentor, Moses. He worked hand in glove with Moses; he witnessed the patriarch's gifts in action and learned the subtleties of his demeanor. When Joshua led Israel against the Amalekites, he saw Moses standing on the high hill, his hands raised up to God as the battle raged (see Exod. 17:11-12). Joshua saw how the position of Moses' hands directly impacted the battle. Joshua accompanied Moses to the mountain of God where Moses and the Lord were to meet (see Exod. 24:13) and accompanied him back to camp. Joshua heard Moses' warnings to the Israelites. Joshua joined Moses when he went to the tent of meeting in the wilderness and met with God face to face. Imagine the things Joshua witnessed! No wonder he remained in the tent of meeting after Moses returned to the camp (see Exod. 33:8-11). No doubt, Joshua studied his mentor's ways and became familiar with his temperament.

tem·per·a·ment

The combination of mental, physical, and emotional traits of a person; natural predisposition....[7]

The doma has been fashioned for the work by God so that he or she has the necessary internal resources and skill sets needed to accomplish the assignment. For example, prophets are pre-built with the internal constitution (temperament) that enables them to perceive and address the condition of the Body in relation to God's eternal purpose. They do this in a way that commands attention, motivates a response, and facilitates change. The prophet is not wishy-washy. He or she does not withdraw from truth-telling or avoid godly confrontation. The prophet has the internal constitution and grooming to effectively equip others and deal with situations as they arise.

The apostle, prophet, evangelist, pastor, and teacher all have an internal constitution suitable to the demands of their assignments. That is not to say that the doma leaves the womb 100 percent prepared to be effective. We will see in detail later that the doma is a person who must be groomed by God to fully become the gift.

If the doma is pre-built for his or her function, why is grooming necessary? Does God create incomplete prophets, apostles, etc.? No. God's creation of the doma is not lacking. The fact is that temperament can only be revealed fully over time and in the context of relationship. For example, until you are exposed to a room full of strangers, you cannot know for sure whether you are an introvert or extrovert. Calling yourself an extrovert before you have been exposed to interaction with others would be like assessing the quality of your voice on the basis of the solos you sing in the shower.

The grooming process helps the doma recognize his or her inborn temperament and corresponding life purpose. It also serves to clean up the damage life does to every human being. Even the redeemed and the highly gifted need the sanctifying work of the Holy Spirit to strip away the residue left by trauma, disappointment, and rejection. Although we are new creations, each of us has been programmed by old "scripts" that tell us we are unable...inadequate...unprepared...unloved. These scripts affect our interaction with others and therefore, our ability to obey the Lord and lead others.

This was certainly true of God's faithful deliverer, Moses. Anger ran like a hot filament through his life. Forty years before his burning-bush experience, Moses murdered an Egyptian for beating an Israelite (see Exod. 2:11-12). After his commissioning, Moses became so angered at Israel's idolatrous ways that he smashed to pieces the stone tablets engraved by very the finger of God (see Exod. 32:15-19). Moses also became angry over the people's murmuring and disobeyed God's instructions as a result (see Num. 20:1-13). His double striking of the rock kept him from crossing the Jordan with the people who followed him for four decades!

We will learn more about God's dealings with Moses and how they ensured the completion of his mission, even if he did not enter the Promised Land. Moses' story shows that there is no perfect doma. Although we need to embrace our God-given temperaments and honor His intent in making us the way He did, we must also allow God to deal with any distortions that detract from our destinies and His eternal purpose.

> *Do not despise the chastening of the Lord, nor be discouraged when you are rebuked by Him; for whom the Lord loves He chastens, and scourges every son whom He receives* (Hebrews 12:5-6 NKJV).

> *My son, do not reject the discipline of the Lord, or loathe His reproof, for whom the Lord loves He reproves, even as a father, the son in whom he delights* (Proverbs 3:11-12).

> *...God is light, and in Him there is no darkness at all. If we say that we have fellowship with Him and yet walk in the darkness, we lie and do not practice the truth; but if we walk in the light as He Himself is in the light, we have fellowship with one another, and the blood of Jesus His Son cleanses us from all sin* (1 John 1:5-7).

Five "Fingers"

The fivefold ministry is often compared to the fingers of a human hand: the apostle is the thumb; the prophet is the pointer; the evangelist is the middle finger; the pastor is the ring finger; and the teacher is the pinky. It is an apt analogy, in that the hand symbolizes work and fingers are God's design to render the hand useful.

The apostle, or thumb, is the only finger adept at touching all the others. The thumb is integrally involved in all the hand does and facilitates much of its function. The apostle deals with and works with the other doma gifts in establishing the Church. Apostles typically have experience serving in the remaining four capacities.

The prophet, or pointer finger, is the "building inspector" who points out truth, areas of disrepair, and God's eternal purpose. The prophet often foretells that which is to come, but just as often reveals the spiritual nature and meaning of current circumstances. He or she also anticipates directional shifts in the Body of Christ.

The evangelist, or middle finger, juts out beyond the others because the evangelist reaches beyond the Church to the unsaved. Evangelists often venture into unknown or unfamiliar territory in order to restore the lost to the family of God.

The pastor, or ring finger, is symbolically married to the sheep. He or she provides the flock with spiritual nourishment, sound counsel, and protection from wolves. Pastors love and are devoted to the Body and seek to serve their flocks according to Christ's example.

The teacher, or pinky, brings balance to the rest of the hand. Teachers inject and ensure the upkeep of sound doctrine, thereby establishing the balanced truth needed for individual and Church health.

Five "Fingers," Five Perspectives

Each member of the fivefold ministry displays a unique temperament and perspective. Consider the apostolic preaching of the cross. Like all else the apostle undertakes, it is "big picture" in its orientation. When apostles preach the cross, they cover all there is from Good Friday to the resurrection and beyond.

By contrast, the evangelist preaches the Friday portion of the finished work. Evangelists are concerned with leading people to Jesus. They easily draw large crowds, but they are not built to sustain the churches that result from their work. Evangelists wisely leave the establishment of churches to apostles and prophets and are more than happy to let shepherds handle the long-term care of the sheep.

Q: Are aggressive forms of evangelism warranted in our day?

A: The Western mind-set is increasingly hostile to the Gospel. We need to be *"wise as serpents and harmless as doves"* (Matt. 10:16 NKJV) and ask God to lead us to those whose hearts He is already preparing. Instead of using aggressive techniques to recruit souls, allow prayer to break the fallow ground. If we will meet people where they are, we will afford them the opportunity to taste the sweetness of the Gospel of Jesus Christ.

The distinctions among the fivefold ministry gifts cannot be chosen by the ministers; they are written into the doma's DNA. Each doma gift is wired for a particular type of Kingdom work. Although the doma's natural predispositions are purposeful, the individual must learn to use these tendencies to advantage while guarding against any inherent pitfalls.

Taking the example of the evangelist a step further, the desire to bring the lost to the foot of the cross can be taken to an unsound extreme in which the decision at the altar is mistakenly seen as the end of God's work. The evangelist and, by extension, those under the evangelist's influence, can lose sight of the fact that salvation is not just a decision, but a revelation. This is not to say that the sinner is saved over a period of time, but matured over time. The idea is that even the decision made at the altar came via the quickening of the Holy Spirit, who revealed the sinner's need for salvation.

Jesus' own statements reflect this truth:

> *"No one comes to the Father, but through Me"* (John 14:6)...

> *"No one knows the Son, except the Father; nor does anyone know the Father, except the Son, and anyone to whom the Son wills to reveal Him"* (Matthew 11:27)...

> *"You did not choose Me, but I chose you..."* (John 15:16).

Fivefold Reflection of Christ

The five doma gifts were given by Christ and originate in Him. He is the embodiment of all five, and each displays an element of His genius, also known as *temperament*. After all, Jesus is the One appointed to *"fill all things"* (Eph. 4:10). God *"put all things in subjection under His feet, and gave Him as head over all things to the church, which is His body, the fullness of Him who fills all in all"* (Eph. 1:22-23).

> **ge·nius**
>
> ...a strong leaning or inclination...a peculiar, distinctive, or identifying character or spirit...a personification or embodiment especially of a quality or condition...a single strongly marked capacity or aptitude[8]

Christ, who *is* grace, cannot be fully expressed in a single office. His genius is manifold; it takes five doma gifts to begin to express His nature. Christ contains and extends unending provision for the Body, in part by the giving of spiritual gifts. This divine supply continues from generation to generation. It is a purposeful release of His ultimate genius that empowers His Body to carry out the work of the ministry.

Jesus' genius is reflected in His Church *and* in the world He created. There is no form of excellence that did not originate in Him. Whether it is the athleticism of Michael Jordan, the artistry of Yo-Yo Ma, or the intellectual capacity of Albert Einstein, all genius derives from Christ Himself.

Shared Doma Traits

As different as the apostle is from the evangelist, or the prophet from the pastor, all doma gifts share within their distinct temperaments certain fundamental characteristics that ensure effectiveness in their callings.

Notice that the qualities listed in the chart below reflect the doma's relationship with God (and His eternal purpose) and also shape the doma's interaction with other members of the Body of Christ. Because their roles originate in Christ and reflect His genius, all fivefold ministry gifts are positions of servant-leadership, created to mature God's people and equip the Church.

ADDITIONAL CHARACTERISTICS OF APOSTLES, PROPHETS, EVANGELISTS, PASTORS, AND TEACHERS (THE DOMA GIFTS)

They awaken awareness in others.

They equip the Body of Christ.

They blaze trails that lead to intended outcomes.

They are strategic and see the big picture of God's eternal purpose.

They attract co-laborers who devise and lend support to tactical plans that ensure fulfillment of the strategic vision.

They have a clear sense of cause and effect that undergirds their effectiveness and empowers them to remedy shortcomings.

They understand the fruits of their labor and how those fruits are tied to God's eternal purpose.

Although it is taught in some sectors that everyone is gifted to operate in at least one area of the fivefold ministry, this is not so. Not everyone is a doma. Ephesians 4:11 says that God gave *some* as apostles, prophets, and so forth. These are works of the Spirit, not the flesh. You cannot train yourself to become an apostle, for example. No matter how many degrees you earn or how many books you read about apostolic ministry, if you are not called to the office of the apostle and have not been groomed (by anointing and formation), as a true apostle, you will not function at the level of genius reserved for the office—and neither will those to whom you minister in the Body of Christ be built up as God desires.

Q: Do all of us reflect aspects of the ascension gifts?

A: While anyone can exhibit tendencies we commonly associate with one or more of the ascension gifts, not everyone is pre-built by God to function in the full genius of a doma. The further suggestion that someone can be called as an apostle of business, for example, also defies the biblical model. Apostles, prophets, and evangelists preach Christ; pastors model Christ; teachers teach Christ. These biblical offices are not secular. Nevertheless, all believers *are* called to influence secular environments by using their gifts, talents, and abilities.

God's calling of the doma is a spiritual and practical act. Imagine if every believer were called to the fivefold ministry. Who would carry out the tactical measures that lead to fulfillment of the strategic mission? Who would see to it that the adjustments called for by the apostles and prophets were made manifest, not only in leadership quarters but throughout the church organization? Who would serve in the pantries and soup kitchens that bring the love of Christ to the needy? Who would see to it that the church's bills are paid on time and flights and accommodations are in order for the apostle's overseas church-planting missions?

In the Kingdom, the most important and rewarding role for the individual is the role he or she has been called by God to play. Whether one is called to the fivefold ministry or to visit the sick and hurting, faithfulness and fulfillment of the mission are pleasing to God and gratifying to the one called. Paul's "body analogy" expresses this facet of God's "economy" so well:

> For the body is not one member, but many. If the foot should say, "Because I am not a hand, I am not a part of the body," it is not for this reason any the less a part of the body. And if the ear should say, "Because I am not an eye, I am not a part of the body," it is not for this reason any the less a part of the body. If the whole body were an eye, where would the hearing be? If the whole were hearing, where would the sense of smell be? But now God has placed the members, each one of them, in the body, just as He desired. And if they were all one member, where would the body be? But now there are many members, but one body. And the eye cannot say to the hand, "I have no need of you"; or again the head to the feet, "I have no need of you" (1 Corinthians 12:14-21).

Pinpoint the Prophetic

1. How does our discussion of ascension gifts mesh with or conflict with your existing views on the topic?

2. Explain in your own words how the ascension and the events of the Day of Pentecost played a part in the establishment of the ascension gifts. How do these points compare or contrast with your long-held views?

3. Consider a friend or minister who displays strong prophetic tendencies. How are these tendencies manifested? In your opinion, is this person operating in the charismata or the office of prophet? Explain.

4. Think of someone you know who is called to and operating
    in a fivefold ministry office. What general qualities of tem-
    perament (the genius that originates in Christ and is appar-
    ent to others) are evident in this person's ministry?

5. Consider a doma gift whose ministry you witness on a reg-
    ular basis. Describe how this individual awakens awareness
    in you or has successfully attracted you as a co-laborer in
    support of his or her strategic vision. Describe a trail you
    have seen this leader blaze.

Chapter 4

The Ascension Gifts—Part II

*He who receives you receives Me, and he who receives
Me receives Him who sent Me* (MATTHEW 10:40).

AFTER MINISTERING HEALING TO THE LAME BEGGAR AT THE GATE
Beautiful, Peter preached a message of repentance and called those who had
rejected Christ to reconsider. Peter urged, *"Therefore repent and return, that
your sins may be wiped away, in order that times of refreshing may come from
the presence of the Lord; and that He may send Jesus, the Christ appointed for
you"* (Acts 3:19-20).

Peter's choice of words is peculiar: *"that He may send Jesus."* The apostle
seems to suggest that the appointed Christ had not yet been sent. But hadn't
He already come? Been crucified? Resurrected? Ascended? Wasn't He already
seated at the right hand of the Father? Weren't Peter's ministry and newfound
boldness a result of Christ's already finished work?

Absolutely! Jesus left no aspect of His work dangling. But until His work
is embraced and appropriated by the unredeemed, the finished work of the
cross remains to them an idea seen from afar. But the instant the lost soul
arrives at the foot of the cross and receives the Savior, a transaction occurs
in the present tense. To those who hear His testimony for the first time, the
Sent One has come anew.

Encounters between Christ and the lost often involve third parties—
human vessels who minister in His name. Whether through an evangelist

on a platform in Africa or a neighbor who shares Christ over a picket fence, Christ is "sent" wherever and whenever a member of the Body shares His testimony. Paul explained this aspect of God's economy:

> *"Whoever will call upon the name of the Lord will be saved." How then shall they call upon Him in whom they have not believed? And how shall they believe in Him whom they have not heard? And how shall they hear without a preacher? And* ***how shall they preach unless they are sent?...*** (Romans 10:13-15).

When the sent one named Peter addressed the crowd at the portico of Solomon, he stood as one commissioned by Christ to steward the mystery, proclaim Christ, bless the people, and lead them to repentance and restoration. He stood as an oracle, his voice giving expression to truth. Peter, the quintessential fisherman, drew many souls into the net. They in turn became *"fishers of men"* (Matt. 4:19; Mark 1:17) who carried the Gospel to others.

Peter's apostolic gift set in motion a cycle of sending that continues today. Those who received Peter, and those who received the ones sent out after him, received the One who sent them all (see Matt. 10:40).

Sent Ones

The word translated "send" in Peter's message is the Greek word *apostello,* which means "set apart" or "send out."[1] Jesus is *the* Sent One, the model for all who are sent in His name.

Prophetic and Apostolic Basics

In Chapter 2, we touched on the idea that, in regard to the ascension (or doma) gifts, *the message and the messenger are one.* It is true that God raises up voices in every generation, but His prophets are more than mere mouthpieces, as we will see later. The ascension gift is created and groomed to be a living manifestation of the message.

Apostles and Prophets Linked

Although we are focused on the prophetic and particularly the office of the prophet, we cannot see the prophetic accurately in the absence of the apostolic. The two are inextricably linked to the building and maintenance of the household of God. The Church was *"built on the foundation of the apostles and prophets"* (Eph. 2:20). Apostles and prophets work in tandem to fulfill their respective roles.

If the apostle builds a structure, but no one inspects it regularly, it will degrade. If the prophet is not accountable to the builder or lacks a clear sense of the blueprint, the prophetic assessment of the "building materials" will be skewed, producing distortion rather than resolution. The spiritual symbiosis between apostle and prophet is critical to the healthy development of the Body and the progressive fulfillment of its goals.

As we discuss particular prophets under the Old and New Covenants, we will see that apostle and prophet are often embodied in the same individual. In Deuteronomy 18:15, Moses referred to himself as a prophet, yet his work was also apostolic in nature. In Exodus 3:10, God told Moses, *"Come now, and I will send you to Pharaoh, so that you may bring My people, the sons of Israel, out of Egypt."* This was an apostolic mission, centuries before Christ. Moses was sent to function at a high level of authority to deal directly with the leader of an ancient superpower. He was also assigned to build a national identity among millions of slaves whose identity as a people had been pulverized under the weight of oppression.

Moses was *sent.* The verb translated "send" in Exodus 3:10 is the Hebrew word *shalach,* variously meaning "to send away, for, or out."[2] Here the meaning involves sending out.[3] To be sent implies that there is a Sender. Moses was sent by God Himself to Pharaoh, a type of unbelieving peoples and idol worshipers—a world in opposition to the living God. Imagine the implications of his assignment! It is no wonder Moses expressed his misgivings to God (see Exod. 4:1,10).

Despite his insecurities, Moses serves as metaphor, an Old Testament picture of God's plan for the Church Age. Just as Moses was sent to Pharaoh, God's modern representatives are sent to unbelieving peoples and regions to release the revelation of Jesus Christ.

*...be blameless and innocent, children of God above reproach in
the midst of a crooked and perverse generation, among whom
you appear as lights in the world...* (Philippians 2:15).

Function Versus Title

There is an area of misunderstanding in the Church concerning doma
identity. Remember, the doma does not *have* a gift; the doma *is* the gift. Our
earlier comparison of the ascension gifts to the five fingers on a hand implies
five separate but related parts functioning as a whole. Each finger is built
differently and functions in a unique way. As individual as the fingers are, it
is their combined function that renders the hand useful.

The doma gift is all about function; when you are around an apostle,
you see how an apostle functions. In the true ascension gift, function is
evident and speaks for itself. There is no need to strain for a title or any
other artifice. There is no drive to validate identity, because the person is
the gift. Ironically, insistence on a title (*i.e.,* the need to be validated) serves
to betray an underlying sense of unworthiness, as though God's calling were
not enough, or as though it were possible that His calling were an error or
unexplained coincidence.

*The doma's function speaks for itself. There is no need
to strain for a title and no drive to validate identity.*

Unfortunately, titles are common in the Church. Some ministers intro-
duce themselves as Apostle John Doe or Prophet Mary Smith. It is as though
their *being* and *doing* were not integrated as God planned, leaving them in
want of approval and feeling the need to perform. This tendency is not biblical. It certainly was not the approach of Paul, the quintessential apostle
and prophet. He never questioned or shunned his identity or played the false
humility game. Neither did he wrap himself in titles. Paul knew who he was
and simply stated, *"I was appointed a preacher and an apostle and a teacher"*
(2 Tim. 1:11) and *"I was appointed a preacher and an apostle"* (1 Tim. 2:7).

Not Apostle Paul of Tarsus, but Paul, an apostle. Is this distinction
important? The answer is *yes,* because the gift is about function, and

anything that obfuscates function must be avoided. The need for validation is based in falsehood and creates a religious "system" based on a worldly model—the reverence for celebrity. The adoption of unnecessary titles produces two primary distractions from function: (1) the implication that the doma is above others and should be bowed down to (figuratively, at best), and (2) the distorted expectation that the doma perform to the level of his or her title (whatever the shifting perceptions of such a level might be).

Can you see how this superficial device opens the door to acts of the flesh? Instead of interacting in a pure, functional way, the titled doma interacts through formalities and barriers that complicate every undertaking. Rather than freely operating in and by the Spirit, the titled doma becomes performance-oriented, and so does everyone in the doma's sphere of influence. Just as a little leaven leavens the whole loaf, both the gift and the intent of God become compromised from the inside out! (See First Corinthians 5:6.)

God's eternal purpose is to fill all things. Paul had a healthy regard for God's intent and for his own role in facilitating it. Having previously spent his life in the prideful pursuit of religious power, he understood his authentic identity and its roots in grace. His view speaks volumes to us today:

We couldn't carry this off by our own efforts, and we know it—even though we can list what many might think are impressive credentials. You know my pedigree: a legitimate birth, circumcised on the eighth day; an Israelite from the elite tribe of Benjamin; a strict and devout adherent to God's law; a fiery defender of the purity of my religion, even to the point of persecuting Christians; a meticulous observer of everything set down in God's law Book.

The very credentials these people are waving around as something special, I'm tearing up and throwing out with the trash—along with everything else I used to take credit for. And why? Because of Christ. Yes, all the things I once thought were so important are gone from my life. Compared to the high privilege of knowing Christ Jesus as my Master, firsthand, everything I once thought I had going for me is insignificant— dog dung. I've dumped it all in the trash so that I could embrace Christ and be embraced by Him... (Philippians 3:3-9 MSG).

Despite the weightiness of their assignments, the first apostles found no cause within themselves for boasting. Quite the contrary; the Scriptures speak frankly of their frailties. Although we marvel at Paul's endurance and his commitment to finish his course, he did not boast in these traits. Instead he declared, *"I will rather boast about my weaknesses, that the power of Christ may dwell in me"* (2 Cor. 12:9). He openly confessed his failings when he wrote: *"I was with you in weakness and in fear and in much trembling"* (1 Cor. 2:3). And though we know the exploits of Moses, the writer of Hebrews described Moses' fear on Mount Sinai, saying: *"So terrible was the sight, that Moses said, 'I am full of fear and trembling'"* (Heb. 12:21).

Consider also John, the great apostle and prophet to whom the Lord Jesus Christ entrusted His Revelation. In its opening verse, John referred to himself as a *"bond-servant"*—essentially a slave who serves out of love for his Master. The Lord not only commissioned John for great works, but He also honored the personal relationship the two men shared by placing His mother, Mary, in John's care! So how did John identify himself to the Body of Christ? Did he invoke a title? No. He simply referred to himself as: *"John, **your brother and fellow partaker** in the tribulation and kingdom and perseverance which are in Jesus..."* (Rev. 1:9).

To be authentic and effective, we must be brutally honest about any devices we use to prop ourselves up, assuage our insecurities, or draw attention to self. They do nothing to transform the world and serve only to turn the Church into a spiritual ghetto where God's eternal purpose is lost and the lost find nothing of eternal value.

Prophetic and Apostolic "Glue"

Early on, we read one of Paul's exquisite word pictures of the Church (see Eph. 2:19-22). In it, the apostle compared the Body of Christ to a building whose foundation consists of apostles and prophets and whose Cornerstone is Christ. In the fourth chapter of Ephesians, Paul described Church function and vitality in anatomical terms:

> *Speaking the truth in love, we are to grow up in all aspects into Him, who is the head, even Christ, from whom the whole body,* **being fitted and held together by that which every joint supplies,** *according to the proper working of each individual part, causes the growth of the body for the building up of itself in love* (Ephesians 4:15-16).

Apostles, prophets, and the other ascension gifts are "joints"—the connective tissue that keeps all the parts moving in the same direction as the Body builds up itself in love. If you have ever suffered a joint, tendon, or ligament injury, you know how debilitating it is. Damage to connective tissue is painful and compromises bodily function. The purpose of the joints is to supply strength, mobility, and energy to the body. When a joint is injured, the simplest of tasks—getting out of a chair, getting dressed, and even lifting a teakettle—can be difficult or impossible to achieve.

The Body of Christ also relies on its joints to function; without the operation of the ascension gifts, the ability of the Church to build itself up in love is diminished.

---

vis·cer·a

1. ...the organs in the cavities of the body, especially those in the abdominal cavity.

2. ...the intestines; bowels.[4]

vis·cer·al

felt in or as if in the internal organs of the body[5]

The ascension gifts can also be compared in function to our bodily organs *(viscera)*. Like the liver, heart, or kidneys, the doma are visceral; they perform and function at the most essential level. Their operation is often unseen, yet there is an awareness of whether or not they are functioning because without them, the body dies. Likewise, much of the work of the fivefold ministry gifts occurs in the background; yet the building up of the Body (or the lack thereof) is readily apparent.

The fivefold ascension gifts are the glue that holds the Church together and ensures her vitality. They awaken our awareness, equip us, blaze trails, provide strategic vision, and attract co-laborers to the cause of Christ. These gifts also serve to keep the Church connected to her roots by continually lifting up the testimony of Christ and bridging the gaps that sometimes form between generations.

CONTINUITY GAPS

In any community, inter-generational gaps in continuity can form. While wandering in the wilderness, the Hebrews abandoned the practice of circumcision, an outward sign of God's covenant with His people (see Gen. 17). Except for Joshua and Caleb, all the Israelites delivered out of Egypt died in the desert. Of those born en route to the Promised Land, none was circumcised. Joshua recognized this gap in covenant continuity and bridged it. He commanded a mass circumcision soon after the Israelites crossed the Jordan River (see Josh. 5:2-9).

The Promised Prophet

You will remember that, in Acts 3, Peter preached a sermon declaring the fulfillment of Messianic prophecy. For the sake of the Jews, Peter quoted from the Book of Deuteronomy the words of Moses, the ancient prophet whom every Jew revered: *"The Lord your God will raise up for you **a prophet like me from among you,** from your countrymen, you shall listen to* *him"* (Deut. 18:15). Boldly and precisely, Peter laid out his case: the prophet mentioned by Moses was the Man who, just weeks before, had died on a cross for all. *The* Prophet was the Lamb of God, the now-risen Christ.

There is great significance in Moses' comparison between himself and the Prophet. In God's harmonizing of Old and New Covenants, Moses was a prototype whose prophecy became part of Israel's spiritual DNA. His words were fixed in the heart of every Jew. As a nation, Israel shared the expectation, *"The* Prophet is coming!"

Israel's expectations for the Prophet were based on Moses' words and example. He provided for Israel God's picture of a messianic prophet. Every anointed person under the Old Covenant was seen as a messiah of sorts. Each one was in some aspect a type and shadow of the coming Prophet, Priest, and King. This ages-old expectation motivated the Jews' insistent questioning of John the Baptist:

> *...the Jews sent priests and Levites from Jerusalem to ask him, "Who are you?"*
>
> *He confessed, and did not deny, but confessed, "I am not the Christ."*
>
> *And they asked him, "What then? Are you Elijah?"*
>
> *He said, "I am not."*
>
> **"Are you the Prophet?"**
>
> *And he answered, "No."* (John 1:19-21 NKJV).

The expectation of the coming Prophet loomed large in the history of Israel. It is no surprise that John's arrival stirred the nation's collective consciousness and produced intense reactions. Meanwhile, Jesus knew what was in the people's hearts. He recognized their faith and their skepticism. He heard their unspoken questions and addressed them. He knew they awaited the Prophet, so He revealed His identity in that regard by testifying, *"a prophet has no honor in his own country"* (John 4:44).

Many Jews immediately recognized Jesus as the Prophet and declared their belief publicly:

*When He had entered Jerusalem, all the city was stirred, saying, "Who is this?" And the multitudes were saying, "This is **the prophet** Jesus, from Nazareth in Galilee"* (Matthew 21:10-11).

*Therefore when the people saw the sign which He had performed, they said, "This is of a truth **the Prophet** who is to come into the world"* (John 6:14).

*Some of the multitude therefore, when they heard these words, were saying, "This certainly is **the Prophet**"* (John 7:40).

Notice the definite article *the* used in every case; it demonstrates recognition of who Jesus was. Of course, not all of the attention given to Jesus was positive. While many believed the Prophet had come, His detractors implied that His claim could not be so: They answered him [Nicodemus], *'You are not also from Galilee, are you? Search, and see that no prophet arises out of Galilee'"* (John 7:52). In Chapter 9 we will see just how paradoxical the Jews' rejection of Jesus was.

JOHN THE BAPTIST AND THE JORDAN

John's ministry location, the Jordan River, is significant in redemptive history. When God's covenant people crossed the muddy Jordan, they stepped into their inheritance, the Promised Land of milk and honey. Their deliverance from Egypt (the place that symbolizes sin and slavery to sin) was complete.

Prophetic Voices Before and After Christ

In coming chapters, we will see that a prophet is not a mouthpiece; nevertheless the prophet is an appointed voice in a long history of appointed voices. Remember that Peter said we are *"the sons of the prophets, and of the covenant which God made with [our] fathers, saying to Abraham, 'And in your seed all the families of the earth shall be blessed'"* (Acts 3:25). A prophetic heritage has marked both covenants!

Notice also that Peter went on to say, *"For you first, God raised up His Servant, and sent Him to bless you by turning every one of you from your wicked ways"* (Acts 3:26). Peter was addressing the Jews; he wanted them to know that Jesus was sent to them first. The word rendered "first" is the Greek word *proton,* which means "firstly (in time, place, order, or importance)...before, at the beginning, chiefly (at, at the) first (of all)."[6] Like every prophet before Him, the Prophet was sent to the Jews first and foremost.

As Jesus' life attests, the road of the prophets is often rocky. Although in Israel's history God's true prophets were honored by many, they were controversial figures who were often persecuted, ridiculed, and rejected by people of influence. Pharaoh's refusal to release the Israelites revealed his disdain for Moses and Moses' God. Even the Israelites, including members of his own family, murmured against Moses (see Num. 21:5).

John the Baptist, the last Old Testament prophetic voice, was prophesied by Isaiah who described him as, *"A voice is calling, 'Clear the way for the Lord in the wilderness; make smooth in the desert a highway for our God'"* (Isa. 40:3). In John's Gospel, John the Baptist confirmed Isaiah's words, saying, *"I am a voice of one crying in the wilderness, 'Make straight the way of the Lord,' as Isaiah the prophet said"* (John 1:23). The fiery prophet exposed hypocrisy (see Matt. 3:7-10) and put himself at odds with the religious community. He also chided tax collectors (see Luke 3:12-13) and pointed out Herod's sin. He drew the ire of Herod's wife and sealed his own beheading (see Mark 6:17-19, 24-27).

Perhaps the most formidable New Testament prophet was Paul, the quintessential Jew whose voice reached far beyond the Jewish faithful and was used by God to graft in the Gentiles to His "root" (see Rom. 11:17). Paul suffered persecution on all sides and was eventually martyred: His former peers in Judaism resented his conversion; the civil authorities saw him as a threat; even some in the Church distrusted him at first or later disputed his stand regarding freedom from the Law.

Prophets Old and New

Throughout the Old Testament God revealed His mind to His prophets, who accurately perceived and conveyed it to the people. Prior to the ascension, the mind of God was not shared with all because the Holy Spirit had not yet been given. Therefore God selected His prophets upon whom His Spirit rested according to His timing and purpose.

Prophets were the instruments by which God pierced the darkness of a fallen world. God used the prophets to bear witness to the light and attract others to it. Isaiah prophesied of the day when the ultimate Prophet would shed His own light: *"The people who walk in darkness will see a great light; those who live in a dark land, the light will shine on them"* (Isa. 9:2).

From his post-ascension perch, John the Beloved described the Light of men, which is Jesus. He also explained how John the Baptist went before Christ and bore witness of the Light to those who were blinded by darkness:

> *In Him was life, and the life was the light of men. And the light shines in the darkness, and the darkness did not comprehend it. There came a man sent from God, whose name was John. He came as a witness, to testify about the Light, so that all might believe through him. He was not the Light, but he came to testify about the Light* (John 1:4-8).

Just as Isaiah had prophesied, Galilee was in darkness; the people could not recognize—or comprehend—the light. John the Baptist pierced that darkness as his predecessors had done for centuries. He pointed not to a Messiah coming in a future century but to One revealed in the flesh. (In Chapter 9, we will examine John the Baptist's role further, especially in relation to the Messiah.)

New Covenant prophets are similarly used and set apart by God. From Paul and his peers onward, the ascension prophets have shed light, revealed God's eternal purpose, inspected the household of faith, foretold events, and declared the testimony of Christ. But when ministering to the Church, the "new" prophets convey the mind of God to those in whom the Holy Spirit also dwells. For believers, prophecy is filtered through the witness within.

Although New Covenant and Old Covenant prophetic (and apostolic) models differ profoundly, they share some similarities. Prophets in both camps share temperament-related and mental tendencies that cause them to embody and declare the prophetic vision.

The prophets' genius (temperament) is composed of cognitive, perceptual, and deductive skills that shape them for their role as the message. They are wired both mentally and emotionally to perceive God's intent and purpose in a particular way. It is not just what the prophet thinks about; it is the way the prophet thinks, reasons, and deduces. Just as you cannot earn a degree to become an apostle, the characteristics of the true prophet cannot be apprehended by natural means.

One final word in this general comparison: while Old and New Covenant prophets share some features, the Old Covenant prophet is in some ways more comparable to today's apostle. It was the purview of Old Testament prophets to levy the sanctions of the covenant whenever Israel failed to honor it. Under the New Testament, such failures are primarily addressed by the apostolic authority. It is rare, in the New Testament, to find anyone but apostles bringing direct correction to the churches.

This is not to say that prophets have not brought correction to the Body. You'll remember that the gift of prophecy is designed to build up, stir up, and lift up (edify, exhort, and console); yet the man or woman called to the office of the prophet does all that and more. The point here is that the apostolic mandate for correction is crystal clear. Prophetic correction must be brought with caution, received circumspectly.

The doma gifts are essential to the healthy development of the believer and the Body, at least in part because they support the sending cycle that is a functional characteristic of the Kingdom of God. Because these gifts serve as the organs and the connective tissue of the Body of Christ, we must be vigilant in our stewardship, always ensuring that God's intent (as expressed in Scripture) is being fulfilled and the functionality of the gifts is preserved through the humility of the vessel and our unyielding devotion to God's eternal plan.

Pinpoint the Prophetic

1. What current-day examples do you see of Christ being "sent" to a lost soul and/or through the ascension gifts and/ or through a friend, neighbor, or relative? How is the cycle of sending being manifested through your life?

2. Describe a situation or circumstance in which you have witnessed the collaborative work of the apostle and prophet. What was the result? (If you have not witnessed this dynamic, what prevents you?) What has been the result over time?

3. What is your reaction to our discussion of titles and function as they relate to the ascension gifts? What experiences inform your reaction? How has your viewpoint of these experiences changed (or not) since reading this chapter?

4. Have you witnessed an "injury" to the "connective tissue" or "organs" of the Church as described in this chapter? What was the nature of the injury? What do you see as the cause and result? How could such an injury be prevented in the future?

5. How did the Jews' expectations of the promised Prophet (as He compared with Moses) affect their response to Jesus? Explain. What can we learn about our own openness to God's eternal purpose?

Chapter 5

The Ascension Gift:
Preparation and Response

*Kairos is an ancient Greek word that means "the right
moment" or "the opportune." The two meanings of the word
apparently come from two different sources. In archery, it
refers to an opening, or "opportunity" or, more precisely, a long
tunnel-like aperture through which the archer's arrow has to
pass. Successful passage of a kairos requires, therefore, that the
archer's arrow be fired not only accurately but with enough
power for it to penetrate. The second meaning of kairos traces
to the art of weaving. There it is "the critical time" when the
weaver must draw the yarn [through] a gap that momentarily
opens in the warp of the cloth being woven. Putting the two
meanings together, one might understand kairos to refer
to a passing instant when an opening appears which must
be driven through with force if success is to be achieved.*[1]

KAIROS IS A POWERFUL WORD AND A MORE POWERFUL EVENT. IT IS
the pivotal moment in which two things happen: First, we become acutely
aware of opportunity or potential. Second, we become acutely focused to

apprehend it. As Eric Charles White's definition reveals, the kairos moment can only be actualized on purpose. The "arrow" of destiny must be aimed and released with enough force to breach the resistance mounted against it and penetrate the opening that is the kairos moment.

Biblically speaking, *kairos* is "a fixed and definite time, the time when things are brought to crisis, the decisive epoch waited for...[an] opportune or seasonable time...the right time."[2] White's description of the critical instant in weaving—the drawing of the yarn through the momentary gap in the warp of the cloth—is apt. If the shuttle is not passed through at the perfect moment, the opportunity cannot be recaptured. The lost moment is instead memorialized in the cloth.

The point here is not to compare the power of God to a mechanical or mundane act. Nor is it to suggest that God's plan is so linear as to be comparable to a manufacturing process. The point is that, in every life, there are kairos moments—one-of-a-kind moments designed to arrest our awareness, compel our attention, and lead us into God's ordained purposes for our lives.

This is also true with respect to the ascension gifts. While they are pre-built for their Kingdom callings, every doma gift reaches a moment of reckoning. In that moment is great potential: The individual's course can become settled. Uncertainty of purpose can be vanquished. And agreement with God's intent can be cemented for eternity. It is a moment of truth in which the individual becomes manifestly aligned with God's specific and eternal purpose for his or her life.

But is it the individual's first awareness of the divine intent? Jesus' calling of the apostles Peter and John reveals the answer.

Net Metaphors

When Jesus called Peter and John to follow Him, they were working fisherman. Matthew's and Luke's Gospels describe different aspects of the scene, but both place Peter in a separate boat from John. When Jesus approached them, the men were doing what they always did at that time of day.

As Jesus was walking by the Sea of Galilee, He saw two brothers, Simon who was called Peter, and Andrew his brother, casting a

net into the sea; for they were fishermen. And He said to them,
*"Follow Me, and I will make you fishers of men." **Immediately***
left the nets, and followed Him (Matthew 4:18-20).

Peter and Andrew were professional fishermen. The fishing trade was at the center of their lives, yet when Jesus said, *"Follow Me,"* they dropped their nets and followed Him.

Going on from there He saw two other brothers, James the son
of Zebedee, and John his brother, in the boat with Zebedee their
*father, **mending their nets**; and He called them. **Immediately***
left the boat and their father, and followed Him (Matthew
4:21-22).

John, his brother James, and their father were in another boat. Like Peter and Andrew, fishing was their livelihood. Yet, John and James responded immediately by dropping their nets and following Jesus. Notice also, in verse 21 Matthew's mention that John and his family were *"mending their nets."* There are no accidental or superfluous words in Scripture, so keep this detail in mind. We will come back to it; but first let's explore Luke's account of the calling of the four disciples:

[Jesus] *was standing by the lake of Gennesaret; and He saw two*
boats lying at the edge of the lake; but the fishermen had gotten
*out of them, and were **washing their nets**. And He got into*
one of the boats, which was Simon's, and asked him to put out a
little way from the land. And He sat down and began teaching
the people from the boat (Luke 5:1-3).

Luke's account of Peter's call makes specific mention of the washing of nets. Again, there is nothing incidental about Scripture. The inspiration of the Holy Spirit is entirely purposeful, so keep this detail in mind too. First, notice that later in this passage, as is true in Matthew's account, Jesus declared that the apostles would become fishers of men (see Luke 5:10).

The washing and mending of nets serve as prophetic metaphors. Everything these men had done in life prepared them for their callings, which were scheduled in God's eternal purpose to be revealed in the kairos moment on the shores of Galilee. Peter, the first apostle to be called, was also the first to be called an apostle (see Mark 3:14-16). Peter would become a net cleaner, spiritually speaking. In Acts 3, he addressed the Jews who had rejected the Christ and informed them that Jesus was the Prophet foretold by Moses. His sermon was aimed at removing the ungodly deposits of religion that prevented them from embracing the Christ, whom they claimed to await.

In his own error, Peter also saw himself—at least at first—as a cleaner of the nets in this regard: until the vision he received on the roof of Simon the Tanner's house (see Acts 10), Peter excluded Gentiles from the benefits of the Gospel. After the vision, he reached out to Gentiles and was part of God's intent to graft them into the spiritual vine that once included only the Jews. In this sense, He "cleaned" the Gentile "fish" and led them into reconciliation with the Father.

The apostle John would prove to be a mender of the "fish." While all four Gospels provide rich accounts of the ministry of Jesus Christ, John's Gospel is focused, not on chronology and geography, but on the deeply personal message of the Son of God made flesh. John's Gospel is often the first Bible selection recommended to the unsaved or newly saved. It mends hearts by bringing readers face to face with the loving God who gave His only Son (see John 3:16) and the loving Son who ministered so intently to and prayed so passionately for His followers before His own excruciating death (see John 13-17).

John's "mending" work continued through the end of His life. As the earthly scribe of the Book of Revelation, John delivered the message of the Messiah to the seven churches. The seven letters applauded the churches that were steadfast and sought to mend the deterioration that had already infiltrated the Body of Christ.

Getting to Yes

In both Matthew's and Luke's accounts, Peter and John, along with Andrew and James, respectively, dropped what they were doing and followed

Jesus—*immediately*. Why would these professionals, men so engrossed in a demanding line of work and reliant upon it for their sustenance, drop their nets and follow a man about whom they knew so little? What possessed them to say yes?

Their submission has to do with the callings revealed metaphorically by their fishing, net washing, and net mending. Peter and John had been created for their callings. Jesus had not selected them randomly during a casual walk along the shoreline. On the contrary: Jesus had spent a long season of prayer before selecting His Twelve. He already knew which ones the Father had prepared for service. Jesus did not approach the shores of Galilee unawares. He knew who He would find there, and He knew their destinies.

When you are pre-built as an ascension gift, the call does not come before God's touch has caused you to ruminate somewhere deep inside (whether at a semi-conscious or nearly unconscious level of knowing) about aspirations, hopes, realizations, solutions, or at the very least, a revelation that something more awaits your arrival. There is a recognition within that says, "This is my measure. This is mine to give."

> *There is a recognition within that says, "This is my measure. This is mine to give."*

All of this happens by virtue of the temperament, which may still be unrecognized as the genius imparted for a particular calling. Still, it presses the doma into a place of questioning—a divinely appointed realm of personal futility in which control, adequacy, and contentment with the status quo dissolve. Here the doma is awakened to and longs for the revelation God has already ordained. The search is on in earnest, and ruminations reveal the run-up to the kairos moment.

While it is unlikely that Peter and John expected an encounter with the Messiah that morning, something was already working within them; it was tangible enough that when He said, *"Follow Me,"* they followed without hesitation.

RUMINATION → KAIROS MOMENT → YES

Remember that, in the passage from Luke, Jesus asked seasoned fishermen to do the absurd: go back on the lake and drop their nets for a catch—after their nighttime quest for fish had already failed.

> *And when He had finished speaking, He said to Simon, "Put out into the deep water and let down your nets for a catch." Simon answered and said, "Master, we worked hard all night and caught nothing, but I will do as You say and let down the nets." And when they had done this, they enclosed a great quantity of fish, and their nets began to break; so they signaled to their partners in the other boat, for them to come and help them. And they came, and filled both of the boats, so that they began to sink. But when Simon Peter saw that, he fell down at Jesus' feet, saying, "Go away from me Lord, for I am a sinful man!" For amazement had seized him and all his companions because of the catch of fish which they had taken; and so also James and John, sons of Zebedee, who were partners with Simon. And Jesus said to Simon, "Do not fear, from now on you will be catching men."* **And when they had brought their boats to land, they left everything and followed Him** (Luke 5:4-11).

In verse 5, on the basis of his expertise, Simon pleaded the pointlessness of dropping the nets again. Even so, he agreed to do Jesus' bidding. His kairos moment had come, and he bore witness to it. For years, Peter had been preoccupied with the "business" to which he was called—the fishing, not of finned creatures, but of men!

Futility of Self in the Eternity of God

The kairos moment came precisely after Peter and his partners suffered a failed expedition. Surely, a night of fruitless fishing was a source of consternation. And just as surely, Jesus recognized Peter's frustration with the futility of his efforts. Knowingly, the Master urged the discouraged professional to cast his nets again, this time for a catch such as he and his partners had never seen.

Peter realized that something monumental had occurred before his eyes. Humbled, amazed, and painfully aware of his sinful state, he dropped to his knees at Jesus' feet. Everything that came before led Peter to this place. He had been pre-built for his calling and for his kairos moment. The epiphany was undeniable; Peter's call was certain. With Peter's *yes* in hand, Jesus proclaimed the man's purpose in life: he was a fisher of men!

Please notice that when Peter proclaimed himself a sinful man, Jesus did not address the issue of Peter's sin. Instead, He told Peter not to be afraid. What a seemingly incongruous and profound response to Peter's sense of conviction! Peter knew he was a sinner; therefore Jesus did not need to address his spiritual condition at that point. Jesus had come to draw Peter into his calling, knowing two things:

1. Peter was already engaged in a search, however unspoken, for something significant. God's omniscience was not required to know this. Peter's search *had* to be so because, in the eternity of God, his calling already existed. Peter's ruminations were underway. On some level, he was aware of something more ahead.

2. Fear would certainly attach to such a revelation—the fear of leaving a familiar life to embrace the unknown; the fear of failure; the fear of the price to be paid. Jesus understood and addressed the need, saying, *"Do not fear, from now on you will be catching men"* (Luke 5:10).

The futility of self is a phenomenon common to every doma gift. Paul expressed it in Second Corinthians 3:5 where he wrote: *"Not that we are adequate in ourselves to consider anything as coming from ourselves, but our adequacy is from God...."* Paul's statement reveals that the heart of Paul was being processed by God. Here was a man who, before Christ, was the quintessential, hyper-adequate Pharisee, a prominent figure qualified to serve on the Sanhedrin. But now he found no adequacy within himself and no basis for boasting in his strengths. Self had reached the place of futility in which the true leader says, as John the Baptist did, *"He* [Jesus] *must increase, but I must decrease"* (John 3:30).

Paul understood the source of his adequacy. Therefore, he was eager to throw off the accolades and trappings of his past. As he wrote in Philippians 3:7-8:

> *But what things were gain to me, those I counted loss for Christ. Yea doubtless, and I count all things but loss for the excellency of the knowledge of Christ Jesus my Lord: for whom I have suffered the loss of all things, and do count them but dung, that I may win Christ...* (KJV).

FUTILITY OF SELF   ADEQUACY IN CHRIST

The Response of Moses

Moses' kairos moment of commissioning is as powerful an example as any in Old Testament or New.

> *Now Moses was pasturing the flock of Jethro his father-in-law, the priest of Midian; and he led the flock to the west side of the wilderness, and came to Horeb, the mountain of God. And the angel of the Lord appeared to him in a blazing fire from the midst of a bush; and he looked, and behold, the bush was burning with fire, yet the bush was not consumed. **So Moses said, "I must turn aside now, and see this marvelous sight, why the bush is not burned up." When the Lord saw that he turned aside to look, God called to him from the midst of the bush,** and said, "Moses, Moses!" And he said, "Here I am"* (Exodus 3:1-4).

In point of fact, Moses' experience appears more dramatic to the Western mind than to a Middle Eastern desert-dweller, as "spontaneous combustion was not unusual in the desert...."[3]

Moses would not have been particularly captivated by a self-igniting shrub. After 40 years of pounding the desert pavement at Horeb, the mountain of God, Moses had no doubt seen bone-dry bramble bushes burst into flames and disintegrate before. On this day, however, the experience was heightened. This time the Angel of the Lord appeared in the flames, and the bush was unaffected by the fire. A common desert event was marked by uncommon occurrences; Moses turned toward the sight, positioning himself to be part of whatever God was doing.

The Exodus 3 account does not reveal how long this encounter lasted. We know that some time elapsed because Moses said, *"I must turn aside now, and see this marvelous sight, why the bush is not burned up"* (Exod. 3:3). This turning aside was a form of repentance (*metanoia* in the Greek). However, this repentance does not fit our typical thinking on the subject. This was not simply a turning from something, as we tend to describe the repentance from sin. It was repentance *to* something. Moses turned in the direction of God's actions and therefore, in the direction of the life God had prepared for him. (Remember that Moses had been called from childhood but not commissioned until the burning bush in Sinai. All previous attempts to act out of his calling had failed. Once he was commissioned, he became effective.)

metanoia

from NT 3340 (metanoeo)...compunction (for guilt, including reformation); by implication reversal (of [another's] decision)... KJV—repentance[4]

metanoeō

1) to change one's mind, i.e. to repent

2) to change one's mind for better, heartily to amend with abhorrence of one's past sins[5]

This aspect of repentance is instructive. Too often as followers of Christ we see only the negative action of repentance, which is the rejection of past sins. Evangelists urge us (and rightfully so) to turn away from our sin, the world, and all ungodly ways. This is necessary but incomplete. In reality, the act of repenting involves a positive action, too.

In its larger sense, *metanoia* is an educational term that implies the process of transformation. For followers of Christ, it is a continual learning and turning *toward* something. Repentance involves turning away from darkness and turning toward ever-increasing dimensions of illumination. For example, by His Holy Spirit, God illuminates more and more of what is available to us in Christ. This is what happened to Moses after 40 years of what had become a familiar routine.

Moses' response to the burning bush revealed his heart. He could easily have dismissed the event. Spontaneous combustion was not unusual where he lived. As for the angel and the voice, Moses could have rationalized and reasoned it away—except that something deep in his heart had been working for decades. There was a knowing that Moses could not fully explain; he knew he had been created for something more. So he turned.

Although Almighty God initiated the exchange, it remained Moses' choice to respond, and he did. *"When the Lord saw that he turned aside to look, God called to him from the midst of the bush..."* (Exod. 3:4). Had Moses turned the other way and walked on, had he satisfied his curiosity with rationalizations or concerns about the hour or whatever was next on his to-do list, he would never have become the prophetic and apostolic deliverer of the Israelites—even though God had already called and prepared him for it.

Moses had been aware since childhood of the providential markers in his life. They fueled a lifelong preoccupation, an underlying sense that some aspect of his existence and significance was yet to unfold. Jochebed, Moses' mother, was a Levite, as was his father, Amram. When Pharaoh decreed the slaughter of infants, Jochebed surrendered her infant son in order that his life might be spared and his purpose fulfilled. She went to great lengths, creating a tiny ark of wicker, tar, and pitch. She placed the ark among the river reeds while Moses' sister, Miriam, stood nearby, watching to see how her baby brother would fare (see Exod. 2:2-4).

After Pharaoh's daughter plucked the infant Moses from the Nile, Jochebed was hired to nurse him (see Exod. 2:5-9). In Moses' suckling years (babies were not weaned until the age of three or four in those days), Jochebed educated her son in the things of God, the place of the Hebrews in God's eternal plan, and God's providential hand in his life. Even Moses' grooming as a son of Pharaoh could not compete with Jochebed's influence and instruction, as his empathy for the Hebrews showed (see Exod. 2:11-12).

Everything about Moses' life had prepared him for his desert encounter with the Most High God. His decision to turn toward the burning bush was preceded by his preoccupation with what he knew (however sparse his understanding might have been) about God's plan for his life.

DIVINE PROVIDENCE

Consider the irony: Pharaoh, the man who decreed the murder of two million Hebrew babies, submitted to his daughter's desire to rescue and raise the Hebrew child, Moses! Consider the effect on the child; imagine his awareness of God's hand and the impact of this awareness throughout Moses' life.

Anointing and Formation

In Chapter 4, we talked about the visceral nature of the doma gifts. We learned that the gifts cannot be adopted or decreed through titles or degrees. The gifts are evident; they are tangible—they are visceral. You might not be able to fully explain them in words, but you cannot refute them. The doma gifts demand to be acknowledged.

Everything the doma is and has is rooted in the reality of God's eternal purpose. The doma gift comes only through Him, by anointing and formation. The doma is anointed by God and formed by Him, not as a carrier of the gift but as the gift itself. The anointing empowers the ascension gifts to be effective, while formation causes them to be preoccupied with God's eternal purpose. Somewhere in the journey, even before the doma says yes to the call, he or she is able to recognize and turn experiences with the Divine Presence into conduits of doma activity.

As we have already said, the doma was pre-built for this—pre-built to say yes; pre-built to ruminate on the eternal purpose of God. While most believers, even the most faithful, are preoccupied with the issues of life, family, profession, finances, and the like, the doma is absorbed with manifesting the fullness of Christ and recovering His testimony in the earth. The preoccupation of the doma gifts is unique to their individual mandates. They have been *formed* to fulfill certain aspects of God's work in the earth—and they know it.

The Prophet Jeremiah

Midway through his ministry, the prophet Jeremiah became aware that he had been set apart by God even before he was born. He wrote of His call in no uncertain terms: *"Before I formed you in the womb I knew you, and before you were born I consecrated you; I have appointed you a prophet to the nations"* (Jer. 1:5). Although these words appear in the first chapter of the Book of Jeremiah, they were not spoken by a novice minister. Jeremiah had already been prophesying to Israel for some time.

Our eternal God views events not chronologically but in their totality. In His wisdom and mercy, He addressed Jeremiah's linear view. He took the prophet back to the things that *had been* (including Jeremiah's formation in the womb) so that he could better understand his assignment in the present tense (things that *are*) and better appreciate things that *shall be*, both in ministry and for God's people.

The Apostle Paul

The same clear sense permeated the consciousness of the apostle Paul, as his letter to the Galatians reveals:

> But when God who had set me apart even from my mother's womb and called me through His grace, was pleased to reveal His Son in me, that I might preach Him among the Gentiles, I did not immediately consult with flesh and blood (Galatians 1:15-16).

Although we divide Paul's life into the periods before his Damascus Road experience and after, Paul came to understand the continuity of his preparation from conception onward. He had been a zealous Jew, protective of the traditions of his ancestors. His seemingly inordinate zeal positioned him as an under-aged member of the Sanhedrin. At 30, his appointment defied the 50-and-over requirement to serve.

As ironic and even contradictory as Paul's treacherous ways might seem, it was part of the preparation that led him to his eventual *yes* to Jesus Christ. It was only after his conversion that Paul realized this. It had not been so clear on the road to Damascus, when Saul asked, *"Who art Thou, Lord?"* (Acts 9:5 KJV).

The Irrevocability of the Gifts

In Malachi 3:6, God says, *"I, the Lord, do not change...."* God's words provide insight into His nature; He is changeless. Therefore, His intent remains fixed and the calling of God is eternal. Jeremiah saw the immutable nature of his calling when God led him all the way back to his mother's womb and revealed that his purpose had been determined even then (see Jer. 1:5). The changeless nature of God was demonstrated through the totality of the prophet's life.

Since God does not change, we should find evidence of God's changelessness in the New Testament. Paul's epistle to the Romans provides the thread, stating as clearly as words can convey that *"the gifts and the calling of God are irrevocable"* (Rom. 11:29). This irrevocability is seen in chronology: from the womb onward, God does not revoke His gifts. But irrevocability is more intrinsic than any timeline could reveal. The doma gift is irrevocable because it is inseparable from the individual. The apostle, prophet, evangelist, pastor, and teacher do not *have* a gift; they *are* the gift. The doma's entire temperament and formation—from conception, through birth, and throughout the full formation of the calling—are tied to his or her God-ordained assignment in the earth and the Kingdom.

Conditionality of the Gift

In Chapter 2, we learned that, while God's eternal purpose will be fulfilled, we can undermine His intent for our individual lives. Although the doma gift is irrevocable, its fulfillment is conditional. Had Moses not turned and said yes to God's call, he would have forfeited his place in redemptive history. If Esther had succumbed to fear and declined Mordecai's plea, the fact of her having been called *"for such a time as this"* (Esther 4:14) would be unknown to us today.

As free moral agents, we can withhold the very thing God has given us. If we do, we will not be used by Him, and our destinies will go unfulfilled. Peter described the human side of the equation by saying, *"Brethren, give diligence to make your calling and election sure..."* (2 Pet. 1:10 KJV). In other words, we can be built, formed, and shaped for the work and still say *no*.

Temperament Under Construction

Both before and after the doma's *yes,* God uses the circumstances of life to shape the temperament. Remember that temperament is always revealed in the context of relationship. (This is fitting, since the Kingdom of God is ultimately about relationship.) We don't come to recognize the elements of our individual temperaments until we see ourselves operating relationally. It is only when I walk into a roomful of strangers that I can know for certain whether I am a live wire or a wallflower.

The ascension gift cannot escape matters of temperament. The issues must be understood (for better or worse); they must be dealt with (through God's refining process); and they must be embraced (as part of the calling). God is faithful to His role as Father; he does not ignore His children's issues. Instead, He deals with them in love (see Prov. 3:11; Heb. 12:5).

When Moses slew the Egyptian, his passion reflected his calling. Yet, murdering the man was an inappropriate response at an inopportune time. Moses had been called but not yet commissioned at the burning bush. His 40 years on the backside of the desert (a direct result of the murder) were critical to the cleansing of his temperament. Moses had to arrive at the place of maturity by which he understood that his strengths and abilities did not qualify him to serve. Instead, his commitment to God's eternal purpose and the fulfillment of God's intent—through whatever means God chose—was what God was after.

The mettle of the man was insufficient for the testing that would come in 40 years of leading the Israelites. God had appointed Moses to impact the psyche of a nation. God prepared him with a prophetic temperament able to inspire millions of reluctant slaves with a vision of life beyond the brickyard. Moses had the unenviable task of convincing these downtrodden and hopeless souls to follow him into the future. And what could he offer them? Only the promise of God that had spoken, not into their hearts, but his!

The cleansing of the prophetic temperament also deals with the "organ" of prophetic expression—the mouth. Prophetic types (both the office and the charismata) are by temperament, talkers. They are inclined to receive impressions and speak them out without first processing what they have been shown and without seeking God's timing as to what should be said and when. It is clear that although Moses' anger problem was not fully resolved during his exile, he was *"...quick to hear...[and] slow to speak"* (James 1:19). Moses said as much at the burning bush where he pleaded his shortfalls saying, *"I am slow of speech and slow of tongue"* (Exod. 4:10).

Q: What word of advice can you offer to prophetic temperaments?

A: Remembering that not all prophetic types are actually prophets, there is some general advice that will minimize prophetic missteps. Not every inner impression is meant to be published. Sometimes, the impression is solely for the benefit of the individual who receives it. Unfortunately, some "impressions" are actually projections that spring from a person's unresolved issues. When they are presented as words of wisdom or knowledge, or as prophecy, strife and spiritual setback can result. Proceed with caution, and listen intently for the direction of the Holy Spirit.

We will see more aspects of Moses' formation in Chapter 8. As we examine the lives of Moses and other great prophets, allow God to reveal His dealings in your life. Ask Him to show you how any negative circumstances in your life are being used to prepare you for what *shall be*. Seek understanding about your temperament and tendencies so that you can embrace the person God created you to be—a person like no other.

Pinpoint the Prophetic

1. Describe a kairos moment in your life. How did you recognize its significance? Did you penetrate the aperture the moment revealed? (See Eric Charles White's definition of *kairos*.) What has been the result over time?

2. Whether or not you have been called as an ascension gift, there are indicators (metaphors) in your everyday life of your giftings and tendencies, much as those seen in the lives of Peter and John. Prayerfully consider the metaphors in your life. List and describe them. What have you learned that you did not consciously realize before praying?

3. In which areas of your gifts and calling have you said yes? In which have you shrunk back? What fears are attached to your trepidation? Which fears have you overcome?

4. Describe any parallels in your life to the lives and callings of Jeremiah, Paul, and Moses. What about these men do you find most relatable? How can their stories be instructive to you?

5. Every believer's temperament is under construction by God. Whether you are a doma or not, name two areas in which God is dealing with your behavior and responses. What is He trying to accomplish through this cleansing? What is most challenging about the process?

Chapter 6

The Prophetic in Context

*Prophetic practice, as evidenced in the Old Testament, consists
in the courage, freedom, and daring to see the world differently.*
—WALTER BRUEGGEMANN, *The Prophetic Imagination*[1]

PROPHETS DON'T SEE THE WORLD THE WAY OTHER PEOPLE DO. MOST
of us see our lives in a series of overlays that are added, subtracted, and
reshuffled as circumstances change and perspectives are impacted. Typically
the personal life and sphere of influence are in the immediate foreground,
while the local community, social issues, world events, and so on command
our attention in varying measures day by day. As these shifts in focus occur,
even the realm of faith and our awareness of things eternal can be in flux.

Prophets see the interconnectedness of things; they are aware of the
threads that become woven into life's tapestry. They see the individual
strands and the overall pattern simultaneously. They are uniquely sighted
to perceive the world behind the world that is visible to our natural eyes.
The prophetic perspective is multidimensional and multidirectional,
always moving through time, space, and the realms of faith in a kind of
360-degree sweep.

Prophets are fully equipped to assess the world analytically, but they are
not limited to strict deductive thought. Their spiritual senses reveal what is

behind that which can be physically observed. Prophets are built to readily detect and distinguish between light and darkness. They are not mere
observers, however; they also bring the light to bear upon the situations
they observe.

Instead of interpreting the world slice by slice, prophets see the Church,
Scripture, current events, challenges, catastrophes, shortcomings, the news,
and more in their larger context. Their point of view is God's eternal purpose; therefore, they measure all things against the yardstick of the divine
intent. Because this perspective is centered in absolutes, prophets routinely
rattle cages and expose the roots of relativism. Their presence is often polar-
izing, inspiring shouts of "Amen!" and "Blasphemy!" from the same pew.

Jeremiah was familiar with the fireworks that follow prophets' footsteps.
In Chapter 1, we discussed the harmony of the Old and New Covenants
and the simple blueprint highlighting that accord in Jeremiah 18:18: *"the
law shall not perish from the priest, nor counsel from the wise, nor the word
from the prophet"* (NKJV). You'll remember that, although this statement
was truthful, it was spoken as an accusation against Jeremiah, who heard
and conveyed the following message from God:

> *"Behold, I am fashioning a disaster and devising a plan against
> you. Return now every one from his evil way, and make your
> ways and your doings good." And they said, "That is hopeless! So
> we will walk according to our own plans, and we will every one
> obey the dictates of his evil heart"* (Jeremiah 18:11-12 NKJV).

God decried the nation's idolatry and warned of the coming desolation.
He outright promised to scatter His people (see Jer. 18:15-17); yet, as is common when conviction pierces the soul, Jeremiah's detractors brought their
consternation to bear on the prophet.

> *Come and let us devise plans against Jeremiah; for the law shall
> not perish from the priest, nor counsel from the wise, nor the
> word from the prophet. Come and let us attack him with the
> tongue, and let us not give heed to any of his words* (Jeremiah
> 18:18 NKJV).

Jeremiah's viewpoint was diametrically opposed to that of his detractors. They believed that Judah and Jerusalem were untouchable and saw Jeremiah's warnings as a violation of their canon. They took comfort in the words of David, who said, *"The Lord God of Israel has given rest to His people, and He dwells in Jerusalem forever"* (1 Chron. 23:25) and in the words of Joel, who said, *"But Judah will be inhabited forever, and Jerusalem for all generations"* (Joel 3:20). Unmoved by the sanctions of their covenant, they accommodated sin and used Scripture to mollify themselves and justify their position.

Jeremiah was not the problem; sin and deception were. The Lord exposed the deceptions of the false prophets in Jeremiah 8:10-11:

> *From the prophet even to the priest everyone practices deceit. And they heal the brokenness of the daughter of My people superficially, saying, "Peace, peace," But there is no peace.*

Jeremiah's message was as accurate as it was detested. Even after the siege of Jerusalem had begun, the war of words continued. When the occupation was briefly interrupted, Jeremiah warned King Zedekiah that respite would be brief. After being falsely accused of cavorting with the enemy, "Jeremiah was arrested as a traitor, beaten, and imprisoned for a lengthy period of time in a dungeon."[2] Yet while he was incarcerated, Jeremiah was summoned by the king, not for ridicule, but for his anointing:

> *Now King Zedekiah sent and took him out; and in his palace the king secretly asked him and said, "Is there a word from the Lord?" And Jeremiah said, "There is!" Then he said, "You will be given into the hand of the king of Babylon!"* (Jeremiah 37:17).

History proved the accuracy of Jeremiah's warnings. Jerusalem fell, and the king was carried off in chains (see Jer. 39:7). Ironically, Jeremiah entered the Babylonian captivity a free man (see Jer. 39:11-15).

Twenty-First Century Rebellion

Spiritually speaking, Jeremiah would not find our world much different from his. Peoples and nations continue to wag their fingers at the God of eternity. Idolatry plagues the planet; every day we plunge deeper into the darkness. While most people are aware of the degrading state of our world, many fail to recognize sin and rebellion as the root causes. As Paul wrote, *"The god of this world has blinded the minds of the unbelieving, that they might not see the light of the gospel of the glory of Christ, who is the image of God"* (2 Cor. 4:4).

In Jeremiah's time, deception flourished even though God's people lived in a theocracy based in Torah. Although my country, the United States of America, is not a theocracy, it was founded in Judeo-Christian thought. How far she, too, has strayed! A nation of people "endowed by their Creator with certain unalienable Rights"[3] has denied those rights to the voiceless: the unborn. A nation birthed in the name of freedom, free enterprise, and personal responsibility has fallen prey to "isms" that distort Biblical principles of justice, generosity, and pure love for one's neighbors.

Revisionism reigns in America because the nation no longer recognizes the covenant-keeping character of God. In the absence of covenant-consciousness, we become blind to the sanctions of the covenant, just as Israel did. Even the Church has strayed in many quarters. Some preach tolerance of sin (instead of genuine love for sinners); in other churches, immature prophets mollify congregations, declaring, "Peace! Peace! We are in a new day in God."

What a dangerous place to be! The same theological illiteracy that engenders spiritual shallowness also provides false confidence to unseasoned prophets who decree fallacies to loosely grounded believers. As was true in Jeremiah's day, some of the most blind are those who believe themselves to be the closest to God. Meanwhile, the world sinks more deeply into despair, and God's sanctions befall us.

Prophetic Courage

Though Walter Brueggemann and I part ways on key issues, his insights are noteworthy. Consider his tracing of prophetic qualities from Old Covenant through New:

Prophetic practice, as evidenced in the Old Testament, consists in the courage, freedom, and daring to see the world differently. That difference is rooted in the old covenant traditions, but is brought to bear upon contemporary issues of power, injustice, and inhumaneness. ...It is for good reason that prophetic imaging is characteristically done in daring metaphor, surprising rhetoric, and scandalous utterance, for to do less is to fall back into conventional distortions of reality.

In prophetic redescription of the world, God—the creator who saves Israel and who is known among us in Jesus of Nazareth—is reckoned as a decisive player in the drama of the world. Indeed, God as decisive character matters so much that all other players—leaders, states, empires—are repositioned and called to account.

In the ancient world of the Old Testament, prophetic imagination... conjured a better world that extended mercy and justice to the weak and marginalized. In our contemporary world, prophetic imagination can do no less. ...As in the ancient world, so now in our contemporary world, such practice—rooted in old texts and memories—requires courage, freedom, and daring, nothing less than the work of voicing and enacting the world anew...according to the holiness of God.[4]

In the substantive (rather than nominal) Judeo-Christian worldview, *the* main character is God. Therefore, the authentic prophet is often called upon to refute social norms, practices, and structures. In every circumstance and whatever the secular tide, the prophet must bear witness to the light.

The same courage that fueled the persistence of Jeremiah should mark the New Testament prophet, who is called, not to coddle, but to critique any distortions of God's eternal reality or purpose. Courage is needed, because the prophet must persevere despite societal expectations and even his or her own reticence to make what Brueggemann calls a "scandalous utterance."

Imagine the "scandal" of Moses! He fled the wrath of Pharaoh after murdering an Egyptian. Yet, God commissioned him to bring a challenge against none other than Pharaoh. Imagine the audacity of the renegade returning to the scene of the crime and demanding Egypt's newest leader to bow his knee. Not only did Moses stand up to the king, but he proposed razing the 400-year-old tradition of Hebrew slavery! His demands surely rubbed against the grain of Egypt's collective consciousness and even the ground-in slave mentality of his Hebrew brethren. His intervention was necessarily scandalous; it was designed to shatter a societal paradigm and reorder the imaginations of millions of Hebrews.

It would prove to be a long, hard slog. Pharaoh would not relent until judgment forced his hand. The slave mentality of the Israelites would hang on even longer. Yet, Moses delivered "prophetic imaging...in daring metaphor, surprising rhetoric, and scandalous utterance....voicing and enacting the world anew...according to the holiness of God."[5] Moses brought the eternal purpose of God to bear upon the conduct of two nations—Egypt and Israel—and transformed the psyches of both.

AFFECTING PHARAOH

Because of Joseph's influence, the reigning Pharaoh regarded the God of Abraham, Isaac, and Jacob. After Joseph's death, *"a new king arose over Egypt, who did not know Joseph"* (Exod. 1:8). Egypt fell "back into conventional distortions of reality."[6] More than four centuries of brutality resulted. The importance of light-bearing cannot be underestimated.

Apostolic and Prophetic Partnership

Before we explore the prophetic within the context of the Church and everyday life, a brief recap of the apostolic and prophetic interplay will help to set the table. We already know, for example, that the two offices are inextricably linked. In fact, their gift mixes are similar. For example, in addition to the gift of prophecy, the word of wisdom, and the word of knowledge, the genuine prophetic office will typically move in the discerning of spirits, the gift of faith, and the working of miracles—gifts that are shared by the apostle. This is not surprising since the two offices form the foundation of the Church (see Eph. 2:20) and must continually relate to one another and to the Body.

Although we have described the apostle as builder and the prophet as building inspector, their functions are not mutually exclusive. Much as the prophet peers into the structure and addresses the condition of the building materials, the apostle enters a church and assesses whether the house is well-founded and well-grounded. As a natural builder who understands cause and effect on a visceral level, the apostle is quick to identify the sources of problems and the methods that will restore wholeness.

In all aspects of their operation, the offices of the apostle and prophet must function entirely from the New Testament perspective of grace. Whether in commendation or correction, grace is the stream from which authentic doma ministry flows.

Q: What does it look like when the Old Covenant prophetic model operates under the guise of an ascension gift?

A: There are true prophets who have yet to get this entirely straight. Sadly, there are also some charlatans who are unconcerned with the distinction. While the authentic prophet uncovers conditions and situations that run counter to God's eternal purpose, he or she does not spew anger or judgment. God's anger was spent at Calvary. Reconciliation is His goal. When Jesus read from Isaiah 61, He closed the book at *"the favorable year of the Lord"* (Luke 4:19) and omitted the phrase, *"the day of vengeance of our God"* (Isa. 61:2). The day of God's vengeance will come at the Second Coming. Until then, reconciliation is our message.

The Prophetic Thought-Life

Prophets, we have already learned, operate at a level of penetrating insight, which deconstructs the appearance of a thing and reveals that which animates it. When a prophet witnesses an event with a group of non-prophetic types, he or she can be depended upon to provide an interpretation that would never have occurred to the others.

The prophet is uniquely sighted to see beyond what the natural eye is capable of detecting and similarly gifted to interpret what his or her penetrating insight reveals. Whether the prophet is reading the newspaper or witnessing the dynamics within a particular church, he or she peers into the invisible world that animates the physical one. In addition to seeing, however, the prophet is equipped to discern and explain the implications for the benefit of the Body.

in·sight

1: the power or act of seeing into a situation: penetration

2: the act or result of apprehending the inner nature of things or of seeing intuitively[7]

in·tu·i·tion

1: quick and ready insight

2a : immediate apprehension or cognition
b: knowledge or conviction gained by intuition
c: the power or faculty of attaining to direct knowledge or cognition without evident rational thought and inference[8]

As is true in all realms where it is critical to see beyond the obvious, insight and intuition are integral to prophetic function. Simply stated, insight is an inference made primarily on the basis of one's reasoning skills. If I run into a friend at the store and her eyes are red and swollen, yet she says nothing about her state of mind, I can safely infer that she is deeply upset. That is not a particularly profound inference, but it is an example of the application of insight.

Intuition works differently; it is an instinctive and unconscious knowing that forms outside of one's deductive skills. If the same friend flashes a broad smile, looks completely pulled together, and offers no hint of trouble, yet I walk away strongly impressed to pray for her marriage, I am responding to intuition, a *knowing* that is not based in deductive reasoning.

Prophets embody both a keen, penetrating insight and a highly developed intuition. Part of the criticism faced by prophets stems from the latter. While their giftings are needful, they are also provocative. Western culture embraces reason and is distrusting of intuitive thought. The "pure" scientist sees reason as the only source of scientific achievement and truth. From this paradigm, intuition is devalued and deemed unpredictable and irrational. Any information acquired through intuition is seen as being inherently invalid.

In reality, truth cannot be arrived at through reasoning alone. Intuition is as essential to the pursuit of truth as reason is. Everyone, including the scientist, must engage his or her intuition in order to think analytically. Analytical thought processes cannot produce unless the mind pursues an internal dialogue between reason and intuition. When intuition is denied, reasoning hits a dead end, and experience is restricted.

A practical example within the Church is the development of systematic theology. Where and how can the theologian begin to systematize the thoughts of God? Even the question seems absurd when considered in light of the magnitude of God and His power. Nevertheless, theologians toil to organize their experiences with Scripture into systems of thought that seem reasonable.

This is precisely the rub: Who decides which manifestations of God are reasonable? What if God acts outside of our boundaries? Do our orderly arrangements compel God to operate within so-called logical limits? Of course not. God cannot and will not be contained by anyone. Yet, we erect barriers within our own hearts by buying into "package deals" that demand rejection of anything that disrupts our systems of thought. Rather than question our carefully drawn organizational trees, we discard revelation. Can you see the danger of pure deduction? Our theology can be systematically cleansed of the Spirit it is designed to explain!

> Albert Einstein, the premier theoretical physicist, under-stood and valued intuition. He said, "The only real valuable thing is intuition."[9] He also said, "There is no logical way to the discovery of these elemental laws. There is only the way of intuition, which is helped by a feeling for the order lying behind the appearance."[10]

Intuition in Problem-Solving

To find solutions that address core rather than surface issues, we must be free to make intuitive leaps. Whether we seek to reform the culture of a business or the atmosphere in our homes, logic is not enough. You can probably remember a breakthrough in the past: You took all the logical steps, but nothing worked. Suddenly, the proverbial light went on; an intuitive "bolt of lightning" illuminated the issue in a way that had not occurred to you. When you least expected it, the problem was solved.

Even the seemingly pure process of analytical thinking relies upon intuition to separate and distinguish the elements of a concept or problem and reveal how the moving parts work together. In problem-solving, analytical thinking begins with the acknowledgment that there *is* a problem. Yet some problems fly under the radar of pure logic. Imagine that you are driving down the road. You sense that something is not quite right with your car. Unless you are a mechanic, pinpointing the issue is difficult. But you know something feels wrong. You scan the dashboard for flashing lights, but there are none. You begin to discount your sense that something is amiss.

Pure logic says that if something were wrong, your dashboard would know about it. But yours is not indicating any failure. Does that mean there is no problem? Not necessarily. It could be that your alert system has been compromised. If that is the case, you are flying blind. Unless you engage your intuition, which has already announced that something is not right, you could wind up with a larger problem.

Whether in everyday life, scientific endeavors, or spiritual matters, we need insight and intuition to uncover problems and accurately address them. This is what prophets do. Although the approaches differ from Old Testament to New, the prophetic reliance on insight and intuition remains constant. The prophet uses both and awakens the faith community to the importance of doing the same.

Prophetic Problem-Solving

A problem is any situation or condition that implies the absence of wholeness. When wholeness is lacking, outcomes are compromised. If there is a gaping hole in the fence enclosing my dog run, Fido could end up taking his exercise in the street. That is a poor outcome. I can patch the hole with a piece of cardboard, but that does not address the core issue, which is the integrity of the fence. Similarly, prophetic problem-solving is not about patching the surface; it is about restoring wholeness.

Elisha was a problem-solver of the first order. In Second Kings 4, a widow was left in great debt and was about to lose her children to indentured slavery. This was clearly a problem. She had already suffered great loss, but if the creditors enslaved her children, she would be completely devastated, both emotionally and financially.

The woman poured out her heart to Elisha, who responded to her situation with a question: *"Tell me, what do you have in the house?"* (2 Kings 4:2). Notice that he did not ask about her debt but about her resources. The woman replied, *"Your maidservant has nothing in the house except a jar of oil"* (2 Kings 4:2). Resources were scarce and from the woman's perspective, were guaranteed to dwindle.

Elisha was aware of the facts. However, as a prophet, he was built to see the invisible world that was animating her physical situation. His penetrating insight looked beyond the obvious details. He remained both insightful and intuitive before the Lord, knowing that an accurate analysis of the core issue would ensure lasting results rather than a temporary fix.

The woman's goal was to deal with her current emergency and keep the remainder of her family intact. Elisha's purpose was to restore overall wholeness. This is the prophetic preoccupation: recovery and restoration. Of course Elisha wanted the family to be saved. But he knew that the imminent loss of the woman's children was not the real issue. The deeper issue was that she already possessed, but failed to recognize, the means to save her children and restore their finances! It was only a vessel of oil, but Elisha saw its full potential. It proved to be her key to entrepreneurship!

This is the prophetic preoccupation: recovery and restoration.

Elisha told the woman to borrow as many vessels as she could. She then began to pour out what little oil she had—and filled every vessel she had. Her solution, perceived by Elisha's penetrating insight, had now manifested in the physical realm. He said, *"Go, sell the oil and pay your debt, and you and your sons can live on the rest"* (2 Kings 4:7).

Elisha addressed other crises. Do you remember the servant who stepped out of his tent and saw the Syrian army surrounding Dothan? The man panicked at what his eyes revealed. He immediately cried out to Elisha, *"Alas, my master! What shall we do?"* (2 Kings 6:15). From a logical standpoint, the servant was right—they had a problem!

Captivity looked to be a certainty. But Elisha saw the situation differently. He discerned that the real problem was not the number of troops that had come for them; the real problem was the servant's lack of perception of the invisible world:

> So he answered, "Do not fear, for those who are with us are more
> than those who are with them." Then Elisha prayed and said,
> "O Lord, I pray, open his eyes that he may see." And the Lord
> opened the servant's eyes, and he saw; and behold, the mountain
> was full of horses and chariots of fire all around Elisha (2 Kings
> 6:16-17).

Elisha prayed for the one thing that was needful: *vision*. As a result, the servant saw what Elisha already knew to be true. The solution was not what the servant expected, but in an instant, the problem was solved.

The Problem-Solving Process

The problem-solving process always begins with the realization of a discrepancy—a gap between the way things are and the way they are supposed to be. The feats of Moses, Elijah, and Elisha began with insight and intuition and often ended up with the working of miracles. Whether the issue was a lack of water in the desert (see Exod. 17), the death of a young man (see 1 Kings 17), or the financial well-being of the widow woman (see 2 Kings 4), prophetic insight and intuition led to the working of miracles to release resources and restore wholeness.

In prophetic dealings, there is an immediacy of revelation that arrives without conscious, logical thought. From the outset, revelation helps the prophet to define the problem, which in turn improves focus and drives continued analysis. Notice that as Elisha processed the flow of insight and intuition, he was prompted to ask the debt-laden widow a question. *Discovery* was part of Elisha's process in isolating and solving the problem.

We see this in Elisha's dealings with another problem. In Second Kings 6, Elisha's staff (the sons of the prophets) convinced him that they needed a bigger and better compound. He consented and told them to get the needed lumber by cutting down trees near the Jordan River. The problem arose when a borrowed axe head went missing:

> But as one was felling a beam, the axe head fell into the water; and he cried out and said, "Alas, my master! For it was borrowed." Then the man of God said, "Where did it fall?" And when he showed him the place, he cut off a stick, and threw it in there, and made the iron float. And he said, "Take it up for yourself." So he put out his hand and took it (2 Kings 6:5-7).

We will see later how this passage illuminates the larger issue of revelation. For now, we can see that the prophet approached the problem with a question: *"Where did [the axe head] fall?"* This information was important, yet the real issue was the need for a supernatural solution that fully restored what seemed to be hopelessly lost. Elisha tossed an ordinary stick into the water, and the iron axe head floated to the surface. Elisha relied on revelation, discovery, and the miraculous to restore what could not be retrieved otherwise.

THE PROPHETIC PROBLEM-SOLVING PROCESS

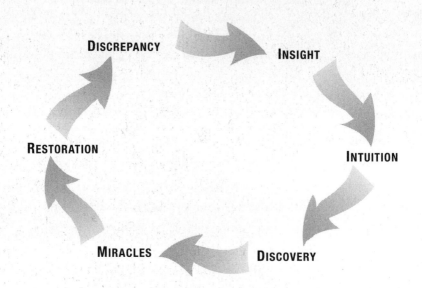

DISCREPANCY

INSIGHT

RESTORATION

INTUITION

MIRACLES

DISCOVERY

Building Upkeep

The prophet is preoccupied with recovery and restoration. In varying ways, this is true of all the doma gifts, which are given *"for the **equipping** of the saints for the work of service, to the building up of the body of Christ..."* (Eph. 4:12). In the plan of God, there is a connection between equipping and restoring. The Greek word translated "equipping" in Ephesians 4:12 is translated "restore" in the epistle to the Galatians: *"Brethren, even if anyone is caught in any trespass, you who are spiritual, restore such a one in a spirit of gentleness; each one looking to yourself, so that you too will not be tempted"* (Gal. 6:1).

The Greek word used is *katartizo,* a medical term. It draws a powerful word picture of a fractured bone that has pierced the skin. Such an injury is painful and debilitating. For wholeness to be restored, the bone must be reset and properly healed. Paul's reference is apt: in order for the Body of Christ to be built up in love and develop fully, any brokenness in the Body must be mended. This is the first and primary purpose of the fivefold ministry: the attention to suffering and the mending of brokenness.

This is why prophets often address troubling situations in the lives of believers. They go beyond acknowledging the pain; they also provide insight into whatever is behind the situation. Prophets provide context by giving meaning to where the individual has been, as well as to where they are going and how to get where they need to be. This aspect of "building inspection" restores areas of disrepair in the lives of individuals, churches, and the Body of Christ overall.

The ability to perceive the inner nature of things equips the prophet to shed light, expose darkness, and remedy disarray. On a practical level, prophetic function serves to cut through the confusion produced by difficult and persistent situations. Through insight and intuition, the prophet can:

1. Help a sufferer understand the emotional, mental, spiritual, physical, and even psychosomatic roots of a troubling health condition.

2. Help a distressed individual understand a troubling life situation, circumstance, relationship, or emotional problem.

3. Increase understanding of local, national, and international issues (whether social, political, or cultural), thereby facilitating effective intercessory prayer.

4. Clarify conflicting belief systems and everyday challenges to faith.

5. Be a precursor to the miraculous, which improves understanding of God's ways and fosters deepening faith.

Closing the Gaps

In Chapter 4, we briefly discussed the inter-generational gaps that can rend the community consensus. Just as the wandering Israelites lost sight of the rites of circumcision, every generation is at risk of shedding essential elements of spiritual identity. Social and cultural pressures, particularly in the context of the spiritual warfare waged since the Garden, bear down upon the faith community. Therefore, in each generation, the fivefold ministry must become personally acquainted with Christ, His eternal purpose, and the doma's specific role in the work of the Kingdom.

This continuity is not maintained purely by training and education. Spiritual continuity requires the anointing. We will study the anointing in greater detail later; for now we must realize that God uses the ascension gifts to ensure continuity and restore whatever may have fallen between the generational cracks. Just as Elisha pinpointed the place where the axe head sank, today's fivefold ministers are called to identify breaks in the Body's spiritual trail. The doma then leads us back to the site of the original loss in order to restore and reestablish the wholeness of the faith community.

The axe head is the logger's cutting edge. Spiritually speaking, the lost axe head in Second Kings 6 is emblematic of revelation, which comes by way of the anointing. In essence, the anointing was lost before the axe head sank, because the tool had been borrowed in the first place. Elisha's troubled logger was operating on borrowed revelation, which is a contradiction in terms. You cannot emulate your favorite preacher or attempt to build your church according to another pastor's plan. Spiritual things can only be built on personal revelation. You cannot hold onto the borrowed axe head; it eventually will fly off the handle and sink out of sight.

The work of the doma is to build up the Body of Christ until it reaches the fullness God intended. Apostles and prophets, more than any of the doma gifts, serve to bring us back to the point where the gap first opened so restoration can begin.

CONTINUITY BREAK: THE GIFTS

Ephesians 2:20 speaks of the *"foundation of the apostles and prophets."* Some claim that Paul was referring to the original 12 apostles and the prophets from Abraham through John the Baptist. If that is so, why did Paul refer to himself as an apostle? And why didn't he acknowledge the order of "prophets and apostles," since, by this theory, the Old Covenant prophets preceded and laid the foundation for the Twelve?

Pinpoint the Prophetic

1. Do you sense or operate in any form of prophetic gifting? Explain. Has your gift been acknowledge by others, especially leaders in your church family? Has your gift been tested? How so?

2. Can you give a present-day example of a prophet who sets some people on edge? What is your response to this prophet? How do you assess the effect he or she has on others?

3. What is your reaction to the discussion of insight and intuition? How has the Western mind-set informed your viewpoint? Is there room for growth in your perspective? Explain.

4. Regardless of the perceived presence or absence of prophetic tendencies in your life, how can you apply the problem-solving concepts discussed to the challenges you face?

5. Do you detect or has a prophet revealed any continuity gaps in your faith community? Explain. What has the Lord revealed about your role in the gap-mending process?

Chapter 7

The Person of the Prophet

[The prophet] not only lives his personal life, but also the
life of God. [He] hears God's voice and feels His heart.
—ABRAHAM JOSHUA HESCHEL, *The Prophets*[1]

PROPHETS ARE VISIONARIES WHO LIVE AND SPEAK WHAT THEY SEE.
Their penetrating insight springs from the light of Christ and the divine
intent. The prophet's vision proceeds from the vision of God.

God's vision impels and even demands a prophetic voice that will declare
what the Spirit of God is saying *now*. For the nascent Church, the *now* message was the fresh testimony of the resurrected Christ. The newly released
Gospel of grace was stewarded by the Peters and Pauls and other men and
women whose hearts were made to beat with Christ's love. With passion
and determination, they preached, proclaimed, and declared the Messiah.
Their words were fertile because they were pegged to the divine purpose and
pathos of God.

In response to the prophetic preaching of the first century, great numbers of men and women committed their lives to Christ, despite the hostile
environment they faced. Prophets are strong motivators in the Body of
Christ; they inspire action and propel others forward. While they inspect

and discover flaws, they do not seek to fix our gaze behind us. They call us forward in singleness of vision and the eternal purpose of God.

Prophets call the Church in the same direction that God calls them. Moses turned toward the burning bush and repented *to something*. He was drawn out of the status quo and into the fulfillment of God's will for Israel. He in turn called the Hebrews out of slavery and into the Promised Land. He kept them in remembrance of their roots in God but discouraged their being mired in their painful past. We too must remember our roots and maintain continuity from generation to generation; yet God's intent is for us to proceed toward the fullness of Christ (see Eph. 4:13).

PROPHETIC ENERGY

"It is the task of the prophet to bring to expression the new realities against the more visible ones of the old order. Energizing is closely linked to hope. We are energized not by that which we already possess but by that which is promised and about to be given."[2]

—Walter Brueggemann, *The Prophetic Imagination*

Prophets facilitate forward motion by living the message. While "the task of the prophet is to convey the word of God,"[3] we should not infer that prophets are nimble-fingered parrots who jot down the words of God on legal pads and recite them indifferently. According to Abraham Joshua Heschel, it is quite the contrary: "The style of legal, objective utterance is alien to the prophet. He dwells upon God's inner motives. ...The prophetic writings are filled with echoes of divine love and disappointment, mercy and indignation. The God of Israel is never impersonal."[4]

Who the Prophet *Is Not*

The Prophet Is Not a Mouthpiece

This bears repeating: Just as every doma *is* the gift, the prophet *is* the message. The prophet is motivated by the purpose of God and fully engaged by it—spirit, soul, and body. He or she is not exploited by God so that the entire mortal frame is recruited for the sole sake of the mouth. "The prophet is not a mouthpiece, but a person; not an instrument, but a partner, an associate of God."[5] The prophet was built from the womb for the assignment ahead. The temperament, cognition, vision...*everything* is part of the gift.

Heschel cites several Scriptures in support of his thesis of the prophet's identity. As Jeremiah wrote: *"You have planted them, and they have taken root; they grow and bear fruit. You are always on their lips but far from their hearts"* (Jer. 12:2 NIV). God is clearly displeased by words that sound right but are disconnected from the heart. The recitation of a dispassionate prophet (if such a prophet existed) would suggest a voice that declares His name but lacks relationship with Him. As Heschel reminds us, this is contrary to the command of God in Deuteronomy 10:12:[6]

> *And now, Israel, what does the Lord your God require from you,*
> *but to fear the Lord your God, to walk in all His ways and love*
> *Him, and to* **serve the Lord your God with all your heart**
> **and with all your soul...**

The prophet most certainly is not called to a lower standard than other members of the faith community. The doma gift is called to serve as all believers are—with the whole heart and soul. To serve any other way would mean serving as one who is suppressed rather than empowered by the Almighty.[7]

Jeremiah, the weeping prophet, served with a fully engaged soul, his emotions evident and aligned with the heart of God. Similarly, Isaiah wrote of a heavenly encounter with the Lord that caused his plaintive cry: *"Woe is me, for I am ruined! Because I am a man of unclean lips, and I live among a people of unclean lips; for my eyes have seen the King, the Lord of hosts"* (Isa. 6:5).

The Prophet, Jesus, displayed emotion—and He did so without apology.

> *Jesus went into the temple of God and drove out all those who*
> *bought and sold in the temple, and overturned the tables of the*
> *money changers and the seats of those who sold doves. And He*

said to them, "It is written, 'My house shall be called a house of prayer,' but you have made it a 'den of thieves'" (Matthew 21:12-13 NKJV).

Even Jesus' emotions revealed the Father's heart and their fellowship. Like the prophets before His advent, He felt strongly about the things God feels strongly about. His emotions were part of the holistic conveyance of the message He came to bring. Even after His resurrection, He was not dispassionate, as His conversation on the road to Emmaus reveals. He motivated the forlorn disciples not to fixate on their Master's death but to move forward in the plan of God:

> He said to them, "O foolish men and slow of heart to believe in all that the prophets have spoken! Was it not necessary for the Christ to suffer these things and to enter into His glory?" (Luke 24:25-26)

The emotional response to God and His eternal purpose is not reserved for the doma only. To the extent that we are intimate with God, we will experience the outflow of our intimacy at the level of the heart. That does not mean that we are called to live as emotional basket cases; but if there is no emotion, we must ask: "Am I intimate with God or only with the doctrines concerning Him? Do I *know* Him, or do I only know *about* Him?"

THE PROPHETIC BURDEN

"The prophet is a man who feels fiercely. God has thrust a burden upon his soul, and he is bowed and stunned at man's fierce greed. ...Prophecy...is a form of living, a crossing point of God and man. God is raging in the prophet's words."[8]

—Abraham Joshua Heschel, *The Prophets*

The Prophet Is Not a Hireling

We have already seen that the prophet is "not an instrument, but a partner, an associate of God."[9] While Heschel spoke of Old Testament prophets, this is clearly true in the New Covenant context by which we are members of one Body with Christ as our Head.

Although the following passage refers specifically to the charis gifts, it speaks by extension of all believers and all gifts. It illustrates the idea that we are more than a collection of useful body parts. Instead, we are members of a greater whole, sustained and informed by His Spirit to live integrated, productive lives:

> *By means of His one Spirit, we all said good-bye to our partial and piecemeal lives. We each used to independently call our own shots, but then we entered into a large and integrated life in which He has the final say in everything.* (This is what we proclaimed in word and action when we were baptized.) *Each of us is now a part of His resurrection body, refreshed and sustained at one fountain—His Spirit—where we all come to drink. The old labels we once used to identify ourselves—labels like Jew or Greek, slave or free—are no longer useful. We need something larger, more comprehensive* (1 Corinthians 12:12-13 MSG).

So, if prophets are not mouthpieces, they are not hired hands, either. They are not capriciously brought "on staff" for what they have to offer. In fact, the process is quite the opposite: the prophet is pre-built to be the message—an organic, flesh-and-blood manifestation of God's intent. Heschel explains the dynamic this way:

> The prophet is no hireling who performs his duty in the employ of the Lord. The usual descriptions or definitions of prophecy fade to insignificance when applied, for example, to Jeremiah. "A religious experience," "communion with God," "a perception of His voice"—such terms hardly convey what happened to his soul: the overwhelming impact of the divine pathos upon his mind and heart, completely involving and gripping his personality in its depths, and the unrelieved distress which sprang from his intimate involvement.[10]

THE PROPHET IS NOT A MOUTHPIECE.	THE PROPHET IS NOT A HIRELING.

Who the Prophet *Is*

Prophets are often described as being black-and-white types. The statement has nothing to do with race; it is a figure of speech describing the prophet as a straight shooter who comes down on God's side of every issue. You never have to wonder what the prophet believes; the true prophet is driven by the heart of God and lines up with His Word every time.

It is true that the message embodied by the prophet is unambiguous and gives the prophet a clear point of view. That is not to say that the prophet is one-dimensional. Just as the truth of God is profoundly layered and textured, the prophet is multidimensional and possesses many qualities through which the message is released to God's people. (Remember that the ascension gift is not a title but a function, as explained in Chapter 5.)

The prophet is multidimensional and possesses many qualities through which the message is released to God's people.

Two words of advice before we explore more of the prophets' dominant features: First, the list assumes the basics already discussed and is not exhaustive. That being said, it overlaps previous discussions of prophetic tendencies. Second, to say that prophets share certain characteristics does not imply that prophets are clones. Like anyone else, the prophet is a one-of-a-kind creation of the Most High. Each has his or her own strengths, weaknesses, and quirks.

The prophet Elijah was a man of great spiritual exploits. He boldly challenged and then killed the false prophets of Baal. But shortly afterward, he suffered an emotional reversal. He fled in fear of retaliation by the demonic queen, Jezebel. He cowered *"under a juniper tree; and he requested for himself that he might die, and said, 'It is enough; now, O Lord, take my life, for I am not better than my fathers'"* (1 Kings 19:4).

Hosea may have been more even-keeled. For years on end he endured what must have been an emotional rollercoaster. God called him to marry a prostitute and love her the way God loved His faithless people, Israel (see Hosea 1:2-9). Surely, this was a source of endless provocation. Imagine the ridicule and rejection he suffered, including the rejection of the wife he had so nobly rescued. She later betrayed their marriage and returned to her life of sin. Yet Hosea never questioned his choice to obey God. Instead, he redeemed his wife at the slave market and restored her to their marriage bed (see Hosea 3).

While Hosea appears to have been a member of the upper class, we know that John the Baptist lived a spartan existence in the wilderness. He survived on a diet of locusts and wild honey and dressed, as Elijah did, in camel's hair and a leather belt (see Matt. 3:4; 2 Kings 1:8). Like Elijah, he experienced emotional swings; he was both the hothead who called the Pharisees and Sadducees a *"brood of vipers"* (Matt. 3:7) and the discouraged prophet who had second thoughts about Jesus' identity (see Matt. 11:3).

You can see that although prophets are pre-built by God with certain identifying features, they are also as individual as snowflakes. With that in mind, let's explore some of the traits they hold in common.

Passion for God's Glory and the Testimony of Christ

The prophet is consumed with the glory and reputation of God as well as the ascendancy and preeminence of Jesus Christ. The prophet passionately desires to see all things come into alignment with Christ. When what is seen on earth is not *"as it is in heaven"* (Matt. 6:10), the prophet sends up warning flares. When the prophet sees the Body in a position or condition below God's intent, he or she becomes anguished. (Consider John the Beloved's aching letters to five of the seven churches of Asia Minor in the Book of Revelation.) The building inspector says, "We need to recover the testimony of Jesus. We need to replace the building's faulty wiring and restore the plumb lines. The structure is out of alignment and needs to be made right."

Preoccupation and Motivation

The prophet's heart beats with the heart of God and His eternal purpose. This is the divine yardstick against which the prophet measures all things. The vision of God motivates the prophet, who in turn motivates the Body to repent *to* His eternal purpose and move in the direction of the filling of all things in Christ.

Grace-Based Ministry

The New Covenant prophet is focused on Christ in His position at the right hand of the Father. The prophet is aware that the work of the cross was a complete work; therefore he or she does not traffic in judgment and legalism but in the grace that defines the New Covenant. Restoration and recovery are the prophet's goals.

Vision and Impartation

Whether preaching, prophesying, or moving in the charismata, the prophet's essential aim is to impart vision—God's eternal vision and the spiritual discernment to see the invisible world behind the physical one. As a person of penetrating insight, the prophet is able to warn *and* encourage the Body. He or she interprets situations and exposes the ongoing warfare in the spirit realm (thereby eliminating confusion as to contrary circumstances). By giving meaning to the battle, prophets inspire others to *"fight the good fight of faith"* (1 Tim. 6:12) and stand against the enemy's schemes (see Eph. 6:13-14).

Sensitivity to the Spiritual World

Prophets are able to see and expose the invisible world because they are sensitive to it. While most believers are aware of the invisible world and can be trained to discern it more accurately and consistently, the prophet is uniquely gifted to perceive the spirit realm clearly—at times as plainly as they see the natural physical realm. This sensitivity exposes the presence and work of demonic spirits. More importantly, this discernment is balanced by the keen awareness of the presence and work of the Holy Spirit.

Restructuring of Imaginations

Prophets from Moses through Jesus and beyond serve to restructure the imaginations of others. This is part of what Brueggemann labeled as the "scandalous utterances" that upend the status quo. These Exodus-like events transform the thinking of God's people and even His enemies (i.e., Pharaoh).

Prophets are often called to shatter convention and restructure the earthly realm with words. Their words function as seeds that are planted and then activated by deliverance.

Interpretation of Implications

Prophets see beyond the dynamics of the immediate. They are called to perceive and interpret events and situations. The prophet recognizes and assesses conditions but also understands the future implications of those conditions. This enables the prophet to provide a constructive context for needed corrections. It also serves to motivate others to act. This interpretative function is part of the prophet's penetrating insight.

The Integrated Soul

The prophet's soul, described earlier as genius or temperament, is comprised of cognitive, perceptual, logical, deductive, and other reasoning skills that enable the prophet to both embody and declare the prophetic vision. The prophet's soul is not isolated but integrated; it is engaged to cooperate with and accomplish the eternal purpose of God in an accurate, effective, and compelling way. For this reason, the prophet feels what God feels and acts accordingly.

Awareness of Suffering

Part of the building up or equipping of the Body in love involves the attention to suffering and the mending of brokenness. This restorative process is the primary function of the doma gifts. For the prophet, it is a form of triage, an opportunity to assess damage and prescribe treatment. The prophet helps to "locate" the Body and its members by clarifying where they have been and what has caused them damage. This in turn affects understanding of where they are going and what will be needed to reach the destination.

Agreement With the Foundation

Prophets embrace the prophetic and apostolic foundation of the Church. They recognize the order established by God for the Body, and they complement apostolic leadership. We have seen dynamic in Ephesians 2 and 4; it is also supported by First Corinthians 12:28: *"God has appointed in the church,*

*first apostles, second prophets, third teachers, then miracles, then gifts of heal-
ings, helps, administrations, various kinds of tongues."*

Righting the Record

Before we close this chapter, it is important to address a fallacy ubiq-
uitous in the Body of Christ. The misconception stems in part from the
damage done by poseurs who call themselves prophets. We must rightly distinguish between the prophetic "wheat" and "tares" so that we do not judge
the God-ordained office by the quacks who abuse it.

Here is the fallacy given life by these counterfeits: it is the impression
that apostles and prophets cannot get along and avoid working together. If
this were reality, God's concept of the Church's foundation would be hopelessly flawed. Since we know that God's ways are perfect, we must instead be
suspicious of the premise.

The fact is that genuine apostles and prophets get along famously.
However, true apostles (and prophets, for that matter) are intolerant of
charlatans. Such distrust is warranted; apostles must guard against wolves
in sheep's clothing. When apostles withdraw from false prophets, the Body
at large often fails to realize why. Because the apostle may act without offering explanation, the Body assumes the problem to be relational. Thus, the
rumor of generalized friction between the two groups spreads.

The reality is that such friction exists only where foolishness masquer-
ades as an ascension gift. I am grateful for the fellowship of apostles and
prophets. They are critical to the continued progression of the Body of
Christ becoming a Church without spot or wrinkle (see Eph. 5:27). They
are what I call our advance guard—our watchmen on the wall who scan
the horizon for danger and for the big picture of the Kingdom. What they
see from their perch governs all they say, do, teach, and impart. Their work
is invaluable.

Apostles and prophets form the foundation of the Church because it
is in their spiritual DNA to do so. It is just as God told Jeremiah: *"Before I
formed you in the womb I knew you, and before you were born I consecrated
you; I have appointed you a prophet to the nations"* (Jer. 1:5).

Pinpoint the Prophetic

1. Describe the qualities that make prophets a strong motivating force in the Body of Christ. When and where have you been exposed to these qualities?

2. Imagine that you have been called upon to explain the difference between a prophet and a mouthpiece. Write out your explanation in 50 or 100 words, and be ready to share it as needed.

3. We routinely say that God uses people to accomplish certain works in the earth. (It is easy to see how the terminology can be misconstrued.) Specifically what does it mean for a prophet to be used of God? Why isn't the prophet considered to be a hireling?

4. Name the qualities of the prophets with whom you are most comfortable. Name one or two who have made you feel uneasy. What was the setting? Was your reticence warranted? Why or why not?

5. Has the misconception about strife between apostles and prophets been spoken about in your circles? Consider the context of the statement, and evaluate its veracity.

Chapter 8

The Moses Model

*Moses was faithful in all His house as a servant,
for a testimony of those things which were
to be spoken later* (HEBREWS 3:5).

MOSES FORMED THE MOLD FOR THOSE WHO FOLLOWED HIS PRO-
phetic footsteps. As the prophet, apostle, lawgiver, and deliverer who led
millions out of slavery, his footprints marked the wilderness and established
the cross-covenantal paradigm for the prophetic.

The Original "Wanderer"

Before we begin our study of Moses, let's follow prophetic history back to
the patriarch, Abraham, whose earlier wilderness experience informs every
believer's walk with God. It was Abraham, first known as Abram, whom
God instructed to leave all that was familiar for what was, in Abram's eyes,
an unknown and uncharted life.

> *Now the Lord said to Abram, "Go forth from your country, and
> from your relatives and from your father's house, to the land
> which I will show you; and I will make you a great nation, and*

I will bless you, and make your name great; and so you shall be a blessing..." (Genesis 12:1-2).

The command of God to Abram seems counterintuitive. How could leaving an established family and the security it offers cause a man to become a great nation? The writer of Hebrews provides insight into yet another paradox:

*By faith Abraham, when he was called, obeyed by going out to a place which he was to receive for an inheritance; and **he went out, not knowing where he was going.** By faith he lived as an alien in the land of promise, as in a foreign land, dwelling in tents with Isaac and Jacob, fellow heirs of the same promise; for he was looking for the city which has foundations, whose architect and builder is God* (Hebrews 11:8-10).

Abram obediently hit the road but had no idea where he was headed. For that matter, he did not know exactly whose voice he was obeying. He bowed in obedience before his revelation of God's identity was solidly formed. No wonder he is called the father of faith!

It is clear that the Lord revealed Himself to Abram; but how? Genesis 12 provides no real clues. Certainly Abram was aware of gods; he hailed from a culture that embraced idol worship. Abram's encounter as recorded in Genesis 12, however, was not with a Chaldean idol. Something revealed to Abram that *the* God of the universe was communicating with him. The voice he heard was the voice of all eternity, power, and might.

We know that Old Covenant peoples received clues to redemptive history, almost exclusively in shadow form. Scripture tells us the good news was preached before Christ came. Paul wrote, *"For indeed the gospel was preached to us as well as to them..."* (Heb. 4:2 NKJV). Abram heard enough of the good news that he *"believed God, and it was credited to him as righteousness"* (Rom. 4:3). What he heard, at least at first, involved his seed being multiplied and blessed in the earth (see Gen. 12:2). Yet he had to have seen something more.

In the first century AD, Stephen provided a clue when he said: *"The God of glory appeared to our father Abraham when he was in Mesopotamia, before he lived in Haran..."* (Acts 7:2). Abram had an encounter with the *God of glory*. God distinguished Himself from the false gods Abram had served. The experience was unlike anything else he had ever known. God revealed Himself as only He can, and the nature of the encounter was undeniable.

This is important because, as New Covenant people, we know that the glory of God is seen *"in the face of Jesus Christ"* (2 Cor. 4:6 NKJV). We also know that Jesus said: *"Your father Abraham rejoiced to see My day, and he saw it and was glad"* (John 8:56). Did you hear that? Abraham saw Jesus' day!

This verse is structured by the *hina* clause, which expresses the thought "in order to." So, more literally translated, John 8:56 says, "Abraham rejoiced in order to see My day and was glad." Abram had an encounter with the Second Person of the Godhead and it caused him to repent *from* paganism and *to* the will of the God of glory! How much of Jesus' day Abram saw is not known. We do know, however, that the revelation moved him and impacted human history in extraordinary ways.

In the millennia since Abraham, God's identity has been more fully revealed. Even in Abraham's lifetime, God disclosed more of His character. We know from Genesis 12:8 that Abram *"called upon the name of the Lord."* After victory in battle Abram told the king of Sodom, *"I have sworn to the Lord God Most High, possessor of heaven and earth..."* (Gen. 14:22).

God further revealed Himself to Abraham through a variety of circumstances. In Genesis 17:1, God revealed Himself as *El Shaddai,* the many-breasted One who can do all things. Years later, when the ram appeared in the thicket just as God prevented the slaying Isaac, the Abraham called the place *"The Lord Will Provide"* (Gen. 22:14)—in Hebrew, *Jehovah Jireh.*

Abraham had an intimate relationship with God, who called him *friend* and *prophet* (see Isa. 41:8; James 2:23; Gen. 20:7). So intimate was their bond that the early prophet bargained with God for the lives of Lot and his family (see Gen. 18). Yet it was not until Moses' day that God revealed Himself as *I AM:*

> *"Behold, I* [Moses] *am going to the sons of Israel, and I shall say to them, 'The God of your fathers has sent me to you.' Now they may say to me, 'What is His name?' What shall I say to them?"* And God said to Moses, *"I AM WHO I AM"*; and He said, *"Thus you shall say to the sons of Israel, 'I AM has sent me to you'"* (Exodus 3:13-14).

PROPHECY: 400 YEARS IN EGYPT

"The Hebrew people had been in slavery in Egypt for some 400 years. This was in accord with God's words to Abraham that his seed, or descendants, would be in a foreign land in affliction for 400 years...."[1] *"God said to Abram, 'Know for certain that your descendants will be strangers in a land that is not theirs, where they will be enslaved and oppressed four hundred years'"* (Gen. 15:13). Father Abraham was apprised by God of the situation that would culminate with the ministry of Moses.

Moses: Prophetic Shadow and Paradigm

As mentioned earlier, Moses was both prophet and (in the Old Covenant sense) apostle. He self-identified as a prophet in Deuteronomy 18:15, when he said, *"The Lord your God will raise up for you a Prophet like me from your midst, from your brethren. Him you shall hear"* (NKJV). Moses was also a sent one. Remember, the Hebrew word for "send" is *shalach;* the New Testament Greek equivalent is *apostello.* Moses was sent by God who said, *"Come now, and I will send you to Pharaoh, so that you may bring My people, the sons of Israel, out of Egypt"* (Exod. 3:10).

Moses became the prototype, or *paradigm,* for both offices. As the apostle sent to Pharaoh, he metaphorically represented the Church being sent to the nations. He was also the earthly "builder" (or perhaps, rebuilder) of the bitterly oppressed nation of Israel. As prophet he was the shadow who would be fulfilled in Jesus (see Deut. 18:15). In Moses God shaped the Messianic expectation of all Israel. Generations of Jews knew what to look for: the Messiah would be a prophet like Moses.

Moses was the Old Covenant shadow who revealed the eternal presence of New Covenant light. He typified the One who existed but was yet to be manifested in plain sight. Because only the shadow had been revealed, the people needed Moses, not only to deliver them, but to perceive the mind of God and interpret it for them.

This was the leadership role of Moses. After 430 years of brutal slavery, his appearance as prophet, apostle, and deliverer must have seemed unexpected to the Hebrews. Suddenly, he and Aaron announced his assignment to God's people:

> *Moses and Aaron went and assembled all the elders of the sons of Israel; and Aaron spoke all the words which the Lord had spoken to Moses. He then performed the signs in the sight of the people. So the people believed; and when they heard that the Lord was concerned about the sons of Israel and that He had seen their affliction, then they bowed low and worshiped* (Exodus 4:29-31).

Immediately, Moses affected the Israelites and caused them to turn— just as he had turned at the burning bush. Before Moses and Aaron met with them, they would have fully expected their enslavement to continue. As Exodus 4:31 implies, they felt forgotten by God. Now they had hope and were thankful to Him. They became aware of His presence, plan, and love, and their response was worship!

Having revealed the mind of God afresh, Moses became Israel's lawgiver, not primarily in the sense of the commandments, but in the sense of God's heart and ways. First and foremost, he became Israel's liberator, which is the primary aspect of prophetic ministry: he was part of God's plan to recover their identity as a free people and restore them to the territory promised by

God to Abraham. Overall, Moses presaged the ministry of Jesus Christ, the ultimate Liberator and the fulfillment of the Law.

THE JUDGE-DELIVERER CONNECTION

Before being commissioned as deliverer, Moses' future role as lawgiver (or judge) was revealed in the question of a Hebrew man who witnessed Moses' murder of an Egyptian. The man asked, *"Who made you a prince or a judge over us? Are you intending to kill me as you killed the Egyptian?"* (Exod. 2:14). The plan for God's prophet, made manifest at the burning bush, unfolded through all the events of his life.

Prematurely Self-Commissioned

Moses' first attempt at being a deliverer failed miserably. The preoccupation of his heart (regarding the treatment and condition of the Hebrew slaves) elicited an empathetic and violent response. He killed the Egyptian because he loved the Hebrews and had been pre-built to deliver them. Moses reacted out of the depths of his calling, but before being released by God to address the situation with authority. Needless to say, Moses' first attempt to save went badly. Not only would he be held accountable for his crime by Pharaoh, but he was rejected by the Hebrew who questioned his role as judge (see Exod. 2:14).

As negatively consequential as this was for Moses, his exchange with the Hebrew man produced a divinely appointed hint for Moses: the reference to his being a *judge* was prophetic because, in the Hebrew mind-set, judges were considered to be deliverers. Prophetic or not, timing was important. As great as Moses' calling was, it could not be properly fulfilled without God's commissioning.

Moses got ahead of God prior to his kairos moment at the burning bush, but his identity as deliverer served him well in

Midian: *"The priest of Midian had seven daughters; and they came to draw water...to water their father's flock. Then the shepherds...drove them away, but Moses stood up and helped them, and watered their flock"* (Exod. 2:16-17).

The Hebrews who knew Moses in Egypt rejected him, but his "liberating ways" endeared Moses to his future father-in-law, who did not know who he was. Notice also the mention of seven daughters. The number symbolizes perfection and completion. It foreshadowed the fulfillment of the Old Covenant in the New, which speaks of the sevenfold spirit of God (see Rev. 1:4; 3:1; 4:5; 5:6).

Decades of Process

After spending his early years in Egypt and fleeing the country in fear of his life, Moses had 40 years in Midian to process his tumultuous past. It is no wonder it took decades to work through all that had happened:

- As an infant, Moses eluded an inescapable decree of death.

- As a Hebrew outcast, he found favor with Egypt's first family.

- He was nursed by his Hebrew mother but groomed as an Egyptian (and raised in both traditions).

- As an adult, he rejected Pharaoh's throne and became an outcast again.

- He was rejected by his Hebrew brethren, who saw him as an Egyptian.

- As a man of two nations, he became a man without a country.

- Self-eliminated from Egypt's elite circles, he became an exile on the backside of the desert.

With every bizarre development in Moses' life, providence and irony were manifested at a supernatural level. In the wisdom of God, Moses had been protected by the same king who slaughtered millions. Instead of being murdered by Pharaoh, Moses was afforded an elite upbringing at his expense. Egyptian schooling uniquely qualified Moses as God's emissary to Pharaoh's court. Moses understood the Egyptian culture as no other Hebrew could. He had studied Egypt's worship of Ra and nine other gods and understood how the ten plagues served to discredit each of them.

Life in one pharaoh's court prepared Moses to deal with another one. But before his mission could be launched, one more preparatory step was necessary.

Moses' Futility of Self

In the seclusion of Midian Moses would surely have done what so many seasoned men and women of God have done throughout the ages: he would have wondered about the meaning of his seemingly disastrous life story. He no doubt hungered for the loose ends to be resolved. He may have wished his reputation could be restored. Surely, he longed for the trauma to be erased from memory.

However harrowing the memories, forgetting would be impossible. For better or worse, Moses could not change the past or deny who he was created to be. He had been pre-built by God to fulfill a purpose in His eternal plan. The call had not and would not leave Moses; it animated his life from birth. Now it needed only to be activated at the right time.

After 40 years in exile, the time had come.

For quiet decades in the pastures Moses came to grips with reality. He no doubt analyzed his missteps, worked on his anger, and second-guessed his calling. Distilled by disappointment, he lost his self-assured, impulsive edge. However genius-driven he had been and however fired-up by his calling, Moses had learned to question everything, especially himself. He had reached the place where futility of self is all that remains.

That was when God called to him from a desert shrub.

Properly God-Commissioned

When the bush burst into flames but was not consumed, Moses said, *"I must turn aside now, and see this marvelous sight, why the bush is not burned up"* (Exod. 3:3). He did not judge the occurrence on the basis of his long experience in the desert. The new, less confident Moses did not rush to judgment on the basis of what he knew. He no longer trusted what he knew. Nor did he trust himself. Even so, the preoccupation working in his heart since childhood remained a living seed within him. Moses *had* to turn, and when he did, God knew His chosen man was ready to lead the nation.

"When the Lord saw that he turned aside to look, God called to him from the midst of the bush..." (Exod. 3:4). God proceeded to call Moses by name and revealed Himself as the God of Abraham, Isaac, and Jacob. Moses was frightened. He *"hid his face, for he was afraid to look at God"* (Exod. 3:6). Then God touched the very part of Moses that had gotten him into trouble so many years earlier: He spoke to the suffering of the Israelites.

With few words, God revealed His plan and resolved the ache of rejection that had wrapped itself around Moses' identity as deliverer. The Lord said: *"Come now, and I will send you to Pharaoh, so that you may bring My people, the sons of Israel, out of Egypt"* (Exod. 3:10).

Moses' insecurity spoke loudly: ***"Who am I,** that I should go to Pharaoh, and that I should bring the sons of Israel out of Egypt?"* (Exod. 3:11).

God answered Moses' *"Who am I?"* with the divine name, *I AM:*

> *And God said to Moses, **"I AM WHO I AM"**; and He said, "Thus you shall say to the sons of Israel, 'I AM has sent me to you.'" And God, furthermore, said to Moses, "Thus you shall say to the sons of Israel, 'The Lord, the God of your fathers, the God*

*of Abraham, the God of Isaac, and the God of Jacob, has sent me
to you.' This is My name forever, and this is My memorial-name
to all generations* (Exodus 3:14-15).

Even after God's dramatic disclosure of His name, Moses hesitated
and proceeded to express concern about his own credibility and lack of
eloquence (see Exod. 4:1,10). The Lord did not acquiesce to his protesta-
tions; yet Moses' distrust of his flesh was precisely what God was looking
for. Moses had matured to the point where he was ready to embrace not only
the Word of God (the logos) but the heart of God (the pathos). This is what
God requires of His ascension gifts.

Moses' distrust of his flesh was precisely what God was looking for.

When Moses turned toward the flaming bush, God told him why he was
called. Suddenly, the inconsistencies and chaos of Moses' life made sense; he
had the resolution for which he hungered. Then and there he was properly
commissioned by God. No longer would his efforts be rejected; and in case
anyone doubted his role, God gave Moses the power of signs and wonders.
God taught him how to turn his staff into a serpent and showed him how
to turn his hand leprous and clean again (see Exod. 4:2-9).

At the age of 80, Moses was primed and activated for destiny fulfillment.

Moses as Prophet

In Chapter 5, we addressed the topic of Moses' preparation and response
as a doma. Now we will set our sights on the prophetic traits in the context
of Moses' commissioned ministry.

Vision

We know Moses was bred with an underlying sense of his place in God's
plan. His mother, Jochebed, had the presence of mind to keep her son from
falling prey to Pharaoh's slaughter. She knew enough about Moses' destiny
to circumvent the enemy's plan. Her decision set up a chain of events by
which Moses would be raised in Pharaoh's home but nursed by her. During

those precious years, Jochebed trained him in the things of God and instilled in him a sense of purpose and calling. She gave her son the information he needed to resist the overwhelming Egyptian influence. The *information* was his prophetic foundation; at the burning bush, Moses received the *revelation* he needed to fulfill his destiny and deliver Israel from bondage.

Awareness of Suffering; Prophetic Identity

Moses had the heart of a Hebrew, as revealed in his killing of the Egyptian (see Exod. 2:11-12). Although Moses' position in Pharaoh's household protected him from the suffering experienced by the Hebrew masses, Moses was aware of their affliction. His awareness reflected the pathos of God, who would say, decades later: *"I have surely seen the affliction of My people who are in Egypt, and have given heed to their cry because of their taskmasters, for I am aware of their sufferings"* (Exod. 3:7).

Moses' murderous act was a betrayal of Pharaoh. Imagine being raised in the court of a king who had earlier decreed the death of millions like you—only to turn against him by murdering one of his people! Moses could not have made this leap (especially not after being educated in Egyptian ways and given access to the throne itself) unless his mother had planted and nourished a seed in his heart. So strong were Moses' Hebrew roots that:

> When he had grown up, [he] *refused to be called the son of Pharaoh's daughter; choosing rather to endure ill-treatment with the people of God, than to enjoy the passing pleasures of sin; considering the reproach of Christ greater riches than the treasures of Egypt; for he was looking to the reward. By faith he left Egypt, not fearing the wrath of the king; for he endured, as seeing Him who is unseen* (Hebrews 11:24-27).

The fact that the grown-up Moses considered the reproach of Christ a greater reward than the wealth of Egypt is a sign that his identity as deliverer had been imprinted upon his heart from childhood.

Preoccupation With Vision and Identity

Moses had long been preoccupied with the plight of the Hebrews and their need for deliverance. Despite his insecurities and eventual attempts to prove his inadequacy to serve, Moses was captured by the vision God unfurled:

> *So I have come down to deliver them from the power of the Egyptians, and to bring them up from that land to a good and spacious land, to a land flowing with milk and honey, to the place of the Canaanite and the Hittite and the Amorite and the Perizzite and the Hivite and the Jebusite* (Exodus 3:8).

Moses' buy-in is evidenced by his prompt announcement of God's plan to the Israelites (see Exod. 4:29). His encounter with God activated and integrated the parts of his soul that had struggled for decades with the passions that consumed him. Now he was ready to act upon those passions and upon God's intent.

Impartation and Restructuring of Imagination

As discussed in Chapters 5 and 6, Moses was called to impart the vision God had given him. It was not easy to motivate millions to leave the only security they had ever known, however brutal and unfulfilling it was. Leaving Egypt meant embarking on an open-ended journey to someplace unfamiliar and unpredictable. Yet Moses succeeded in leading them out—with the wealth of the Egyptians! (See Exodus 3:22.)

The process of transforming the nation's psyche had begun. The process would continue for 40 years until after Moses' death. Immediately following the mass circumcision at Gilgal, the burden of the Israelites' slave identity lifted. *"The Lord said to Joshua, 'Today I have rolled away the reproach of Egypt from you'"* (Josh. 5:9). The prophetic ministry of Moses awakened in Israel an alternative consciousness that was based, not on the past, but on the promise of God.

Passion for God's Glory

Moses experienced God's glory at the burning bush and exposed the Israelites to His glory for 40 years. They witnessed the cloud by day and the pillar of fire by night (see Exod. 13:21); they saw the mount of God covered in smoke (see Exod. 19:18); they worshiped in the Tabernacle (see Exod. 40:35); and they saw God's glory in the face of Moses (see 2 Cor. 3:7). When

God's glory was disrespected, Moses expressed the pathos of God (and some of his fleshly anger). At the sight of their molten calf, he became enraged. He threw down the tablets God had inscribed, melted the calf, ground it into powder, and forced the people to drink it (see Exod. 32:19-20).

Moses was passionate for God's glory. Although the disobedience spawned by his anger prevented him from entering the Promised Land, he fulfilled his greater mission; he led Israel to the place of promise; he mentored Joshua for leadership; and he pointed Israel to the Messiah.

Moses was indeed the paradigm prophet.

Pinpoint the Prophetic

1. Compare and contrast the lives of Abraham and Moses. What speaks to you most about Abraham's life? About Moses' life?

2. Moses' ministry had an immediate effect on the Israelites. Imagine that you were in their ranks when he announced his calling as deliverer. How might you have reacted?

3. Explain the trauma and the prophetic value of the rejection Moses suffered from his Hebrew brethren. Relate Moses' rejection to an experience in your life.

4. Have you had a Midian experience? Explain the context and its effects on your life.

5. Why is it important for a prophet to be consumed with passion for God's glory? How did this passion manifest appropriately in Moses' life? How did it manifest inappropriately?

Chapter 9

A Prophet Introduces *the* Prophet

When Elizabeth heard Mary's greeting, the baby
leaped in her womb; and Elizabeth was filled with
the Holy Spirit. And she cried out with a loud voice
and said, "Blessed among women are you, and blessed
is the fruit of your womb!" (Luke 1:41-42).

JOHN THE BAPTIST

He was the prophetic voice *"of one crying in the wilderness, 'Make ready the way of the Lord, make His paths straight!'"* (Matt. 3:3). The ministry of the last Old Covenant prophet, John the Baptist, began when he pointed to the Messiah from his mother's womb.

Moses and others had pointed Israel to the Christ for centuries, but this was different. John's voice did not proclaim the One yet to come but the One who had arrived—the Incarnate *"Lamb of God who takes away the sin of the world!"* (John 1:29). John the Baptist did not part the Red Sea or spend decades transforming a people. He preached a succinct and timely message of repentance; he bore witness to the Light, and he made way for Him, saying, *"He must increase, but I must decrease"* (John 3:30).

"He must increase, but I must decrease" (John 3:30).

John the Baptist was clear about his role. As John the Beloved wrote:

> *He came as a witness, to testify about the light, so that all might believe through him. He was not the light, but he came to testify about the light* (John 1:7-8).

John the Baptist was consumed with the glory of the Incarnate Son of God, *"the true light which, coming into the world, enlightens every man"* (John 1:9). He came to prepare the way by preparing hearts to receive Him. But Jesus was clearly visible, so why was John called to interpret what seemed to be obvious?

In Chapter 4 we discussed the distorting effects of darkness. John the Beloved explained that *"the light shines in the darkness, and the darkness did not comprehend it"* (John 1:5). Isaiah prophesied Jesus' arrival and described the darkness enshrouding Galilee (see Isa. 9:1-2).

John the Baptist had the penetrating insight and light-versus-darkness awareness of a prophet. As such, he drew people out of spiritual blindness and shed light on the skepticism, traditions, peer pressure, and ignorance that stood between them and God's eternal purpose. John had been pre-built to pierce the steel-reinforced façade of religion; he was created to give new hope to the lost and lead them out. That doesn't mean everyone fell at Jesus' feet; it means that Israel reached a pivot point: the first Adam led humankind into sin; the Second Adam had come to deliver them. And John the Baptist came to *"make His paths straight!"* (Matt. 3:3).

Q: What about those who haven't heard the good news?

A: John 1:9 says that *"the true light...coming into the world, enlightens every man."* God is just. No one will be condemned for eternity because he or she has not heard about the cross of Christ. Everyone will have heard the truth before the Day of Judgment arrives. Whether it came through a recurring thought, a stranger on a street corner, the friendly soul behind the deli counter, or the loving parent or spouse who pleaded for decades, those who resisted His wooing will hear the doleful words: "If only you had listened. If only you had surrendered. I offered all of it to you."

John the Baptist: Elite Prophet

Jesus distinguished John the Baptist from other prophets, saying, *"Among those born of women there has not arisen anyone greater than John the Baptist..."* (Matt. 11:11). Jesus was speaking in pre-ascension terms, as the remainder of the verse explains. Nevertheless, Jesus' words were more than complimentary; they established a bar that is important to any study of the prophetic. Jesus said, in essence, that no human vessel—not Moses, not Elijah, not Abraham—none was greater than John the Baptist.

Jesus is not capricious or hyperbolic, so why did He make this statement? Remember that the message and the messenger are one. John was faithful to his calling, but so were Abraham, Moses, Elijah, and others. The difference between John and all who came before him is the importance of his message. John's message came at a critical point in history—the Messiah had come in the flesh!

We discussed the culmination of history in Chapter 2. We know that all things are to be fulfilled in Christ. His advent was, therefore, monumentally important in redemptive and world history. John the Baptist was the voice on the scene at this culminating point of history. His message was mission critical; humankind faced the most impactful decision since the Garden of Eden. No longer was the Messiah a conversation for someday. *The* day— the fullness of times—had come. The promise was now manifested, and all people were accountable for all eternity.

An Exodus Event

You will remember from Chapter 4 the significance of John's ministry at the Jordan. The river Israel crossed to enter their Promised Land was now the site of John's preaching and baptizing. It powerfully symbolized and prophetically proclaimed the nature of his ministry. Israel was again positioned to enter her inheritance—not in terms of real estate but in the greater sense of redemption.

Like Moses before him, John the Baptist stirred the nation from her slumber. He called the people away from Jerusalem's comforts and into the wilderness, where he revealed their need of repentance. He prepared them to leave the conventions of the familiar for an age of true relationship with the Father.

John's ministry also coincided with Israel's lack of spiritual expectancy. The nation had a history of miracles, yet the miraculous had become a thing of the past. Just as Moses led the Hebrews out of the expectation of indefinite slavery, John led them out of spiritual stagnancy. He reignited the spiritual imagination of the Jewish people, upset the status quo, and rewired their expectations. Needless to say, he proved to be a thorn in the side of religious and secular leaders (see Matt. 3:7; Mark 6:18).

MOSES AND JOHN THE BAPTIST

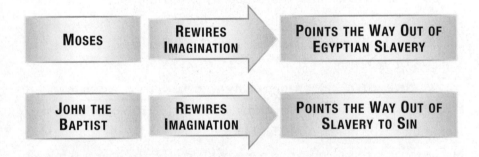

MOSES	REWIRES IMAGINATION	POINTS THE WAY OUT OF EGYPTIAN SLAVERY
JOHN THE BAPTIST	REWIRES IMAGINATION	POINTS THE WAY OUT OF SLAVERY TO SIN

There was a new prophet in town. The conventions of religion and local politics were tested. John enlightened a darkened world to the fact that everything was about to change. A new exodus was in the offing, and John was its interim leader. The Law of Moses had served its purpose; the "tutor" pointed to Christ so that people everywhere might be justified by faith (see Gal. 3:24). Now Christ had come. The "tutor" was about to be relieved of duty.

THE KINGDOM AT HAND

John the Baptist helped the people to locate themselves in redemptive history. This involved acknowledging who they were, where they had been, and where they were now. John's central message was *"Repent, for the kingdom of heaven is at hand"* (Matt. 3:2). The paradigm had changed, and hearts had to change, too.

Managing Expectations

"Are You the Christ?"

Israel had long expected a Prophet to be their Messiah and Liberator. They wondered whether John was He. So the *"Jews sent to him priests and Levites from Jerusalem to ask him, 'Who are you?'"* (John 1:19). Many prophets had come down the pike; none so far had proven to be the One. It's no surprise that they questioned John thoroughly. Even after he told them he was not the Christ, they continued their queries:

> *"What then? Are you Elijah?" And he said, "I am not." "Are you the Prophet?" And he answered, "No." They said then to him, "Who are you, so that we may give an answer to those who sent us? What do you say about yourself?"* (John 1:21-22)

John was not surprised by the questioning. He understood the Jews' DNA; he knew that prophecies from the likes of Moses (see Deut. 18:15) predisposed them to be on the lookout for their Messiah. As a member of the Kingdom's "advance guard," answering questions and interpreting the signs of the times were part of his job description. In John 1:23, he identified himself as *"a voice of one crying in the wilderness."* In John 1:20, he said clearly, *"I am not the Christ."* The very next day, while baptizing at the Jordan, John made a positive ID: He pointed to Jesus and proclaimed: *"Behold, the Lamb of God who takes away the sin of the world!"* (John 1:29).

Salvation and Baptism With Fire

John proclaimed the Messiah's arrival but did not stop there. He interpreted two implications of His death, resurrection, and ascension:

> *"As for me, I baptize you with water for repentance, but He who is coming after me is mightier than I, and I am not fit to remove His sandals; **He will baptize you with the Holy Spirit and fire.** And His winnowing fork is in His hand, and He will thoroughly clear His threshing floor; and **He will gather His wheat into the barn, but He will burn up the chaff with unquenchable fire"** (Matthew 3:11-12).

John saw the Day of Pentecost, although he would be executed before it occurred. In prophesying the baptism with the Holy Spirit, he provided the people with additional insight as to where they were going. He also provided a warning: once the work of the cross was accomplished, every human being would have to decide whether to be gathered as Jesus' wheat or burned as chaff.

Not only had the Messiah come and been identified by John the Baptist, but the lines of eternity had been forever drawn.

JESUS: *THE* PROPHET

Considering the controversy provoked by the presence and purpose of God's prophets through the ages, it is no surprise that the advent of Jesus stirred the region's spiritual and political pot. Wherever He showed up, He garnered attention. The curious, the hopeful, and the even the hateful made their feelings known:

> *And when He had entered Jerusalem, all the city was stirred, saying,* **"Who is this?"** (Matthew 21:10)

*Therefore when the people saw the sign which He had performed, they said, "**This is truly the Prophet** who is to come into the world"* (John 6:14).

*They answered him [Nicodemus], "**You are not also from Galilee, are you? Search, and see that no prophet arises out of Galilee**"* (John 7:52).

As previously mentioned, some were quick to recognize Jesus. They made the distinction between Him and previous prophets, and they verbalized their conviction. Jesus' supporters were not necessarily in the ranks of religious leadership. As is true of every generation, those who claim to be closest to God are often deceived. Religious leaders were among the most vitriolic of Jesus' opponents (two notable exceptions were Nicodemus and Joseph of Arimathea, two Sanhedrin members who loved Jesus and believed in Him).

It is one of the great paradoxes of history that the appointed stewards of Torah and the Prophets proved to be some of the most ardent critics of the One of whom the Scriptures attested. How is it that their hearts did not leap within them as the yet-to-be born John the Baptist leaped in his mother's womb?

RECOGNIZING THE REDEEMER

Simeon, a devout man upon whom the Holy Spirit rested, instantly recognized the infant Jesus as the Savior. He yearned for the Messiah's coming and believed that he would live long enough to witness His arrival. The day he held the Child, he also prophesied the sorrow He would bring His mother (see Luke 2:25-35).

Another spiritually alert Jew, the aged prophetess Anna, recognized the infant Messiah. She had been in fasting and prayer for decades and gave thanks for Jesus' soon redemption of Israel (see Luke 2:36-38).

Jesus was well aware of the rumblings over His identity. After three decades as the son of Mary, Jesus offended even those in His hometown. Their familiarity with His family became a stumbling block; they could not reconcile His claims of divinity with His apparent humanity (an issue that has plagued unbelievers for 2,000 years). They found it easier to question than to receive Him. He responded to their interrogations by identifying with the plight of other prophets:

> He came to His hometown and began teaching them in their synagogue, so that they were astonished, and said, "Where did this man get this wisdom and these miraculous powers? Is not this the carpenter's son? Is not His mother called Mary, and His brothers, James and Joseph and Simon and Judas? And His sisters, are they not all with us? Where then did this man get all these things?" And they took offense at Him. But Jesus said to them, **"A prophet is not without honor except in his hometown, and in his own household"** (Matthew 13:54-57).

The Prophet saw the invisible world that was operating behind the physical one. He read their hearts; He understood the deceptions to which the human race had fallen prey. He knew that He was destined to be *"despised and forsaken of men...like one from whom men hide their face"* (Isa. 53:3). He knew that although He had come to save them, many would not esteem Him (see Isa. 53:3).

Miracles and Israel's Psyche

If Moses and John the Baptist served to restructure thinking and lead God's people into Exodus events, the ultimate Deliverer did it on a grand scale. As John the Baptist faded from view, the Prophet entered the national consciousness. No other prophet had ever seen with the Father's eyes as Jesus did. Nor had anyone ever been so aligned with the Father's will. Even as He claimed divinity, Jesus revealed a heart of obedience, saying, *"The Son can do nothing of Himself, unless it is something He sees the Father doing; for whatever the Father does, these things the Son also does in like manner"* (John 5:19).

Jesus revealed a viewpoint like no other. Where the people saw sickness and demonization, He saw healing and deliverance. Sickness and demonic spirits did not intimidate Him; they bowed to Him. When Jesus healed Simon Peter's mother-in-law, the deliverance was immediate. She left her sick bed and began to serve. The psyche of the city was transformed by the news. People brought *"all who were ill and those who were demon-possessed. And the whole city had gathered at the door"* (Mark 1:32-33).

> *Sickness and demonic spirits did not intimidate Jesus; they bowed to Him.*

Jesus saw beyond destruction and death and performed miracles that defied natural thinking. He planted seeds of hope and possibility and then activated them by ministering in the power of deliverance. Exodus events occurred everywhere He went. His exploits were so scandalous in the eyes of conventional thinkers as to seem threatening to the traditional structures of order and power. With His words and deeds—His prophetic ministry—Jesus broke the rules of conventional religion and created a world of possibility that had not previously existed.

Jesus' first miracle—the changing of water into wine—was the prophetic declaration of a new wineskin, a new age, so to speak. John's Gospel reveals the importance of the miracle: *"This beginning of His signs Jesus did in Cana of Galilee, and **manifested His glory, and His disciples believed in Him"*** (John 2:11).

Notice that John did not say everyone at the wedding believed in Him. The miracle was not designed to improve the party. Instead, it secured the beginning of a new community. *"His disciples believed in Him."* Whatever doubts may have existed before, the miracle at Cana marked the dawning of the True Light upon the disciples. It restructured their thinking and ensured their fidelity to the new community's leader, Jesus Christ.

Later miracles revealed the True Light to those outside Jesus' inner circle and helped them to make the connection between the Prophet described by Moses and Jesus. The miracle of the loaves and fishes in John 6 was just such a miracle. The multitude saw something beyond their wildest dreams.

"Therefore when the people saw the sign which He had performed, they said, 'This is of a truth the Prophet who is to come into the world'" (John 6:14).

The new community was growing. In John 9, Jesus created a stir with another public miracle: the healing of the blind man. Those who knew the man were perplexed by the restoration of his eyesight. When they questioned him, he testified about Jesus, the clay and spittle, and the washing in the pool at Siloam. His explanations did not satisfy their curiosity. They took him before the Pharisees, who were less concerned with the man's deliverance than with Jesus having healed him on the Sabbath.

The Pharisees grilled the man and his family but failed to discredit the miracle or Jesus. Disgusted with the healed man and the Messiah, they threw the man out on the street, where Jesus found him the second time:

> *Jesus heard that they had put him out; and finding him, He said, "Do you believe in the Son of Man?" He answered and said, "And who is He, Lord, that I may believe in Him?" Jesus said to him, "You have both seen Him, and He is the one who is talking with you." And he said, "Lord, I believe." And he worshiped Him. And Jesus said, "For judgment I came into this world, that those who do not see may see; and that those who see may become blind"* (John 9:35-39).

The Pharisees overheard the conversation. Smug and self-satisfied, they challenged Jesus' assessment of spiritual blindness:

> *And said to Him, "We are not blind too, are we?" Jesus said to them, "If you were blind, you would have no sin; but since you say, 'We see,' your sin remains"* (John 9:40-41).

The healing of the blind man upset the norms of Jewish society. It restructured Israel's imagination and created a national awareness that the Moses paradigm was being fulfilled. What Moses was to the deliverance of Israel, Jesus was to their deliverance into the Kingdom to come. And just as Moses threatened the power of Pharaoh, Jesus now threatened the religious chokehold of the Pharisees. The reactions to Jesus' presence and works were mixed; nevertheless, the psyche of Israel had been changed.

MOSES	REWIRES IMAGINATION	DELIVERS INTO THE PROMISED LAND

A New and Eternal Community

John the Baptist played a role in the forming of the New Covenant community when he proclaimed the Lamb of God before his own disciples. We have read about Jesus calling Peter and Andrew into ministry; here we see John's account of their pure desire to follow Him:

> *John was standing with two of his disciples, and he looked upon Jesus as He walked, and said, "Behold, the Lamb of God!" The two disciples heard him speak, and they followed Jesus....One of the two who heard John speak and followed Him, was Andrew, Simon Peter's brother* (John 1:35-37,40).

During this encounter, Andrew identified Jesus as the Messiah (see John 1:41). The new wineskin symbolized by the first miracle at Cana was to be a new nation, a new community, and a new priesthood. Its new government fulfilled the shadow of the Old Covenant; its 12 leaders resembled the 12 patriarchs (Jacob's sons). Jesus said in John 5:19 that He always followed His Father's example. He followed the pattern of 12 because it was the pattern His Father used to build the nation of Israel.

Although Old and New Covenant government patterns were parallel, the covenants were distinct. Quoting from a portion of Isaiah 61, Jesus made the distinction clear:

> *The Spirit of the Lord is upon Me, because He anointed Me to preach the gospel to the poor. He has sent Me to proclaim release to the captives, and recovery of sight to the blind, to set free those who are oppressed, to proclaim the favorable year of the Lord* (Luke 4:18-20).

Remember that Isaiah 61:2 said *"To proclaim the favorable year of the Lord, **and the day of vengeance of our God....**"* When Jesus declared His mission in the synagogue, He omitted mention of the day of vengeance. The New Covenant community was not built upon the Law because Jesus fulfilled the Law. The new community was built on a foundation of grace.

> Through the testimony of Jesus, the New Covenant community came to know God as Father. Jesus said, *"All things have been handed over to Me by My Father; and no one knows the Son, except the Father; nor does anyone know the Father, except the Son, and anyone to whom the Son wills to reveal Him"* (Matt. 11:27). Although Jesus' references to His Father caused consternation, they also created a new mind-set regarding the relationship between God and His children.

The Chief Cornerstone

Now we return to one of the foundational Scriptures in our discussion of the prophetic:

> *You are no longer strangers and aliens, but you are fellow citizens with the saints, and are of* **God's household, having been built upon the foundation of the apostles and prophets, Christ Jesus Himself being the corner stone,** *in whom the whole building, being fitted together is growing into a holy temple in the Lord; in whom you also are being built together into a dwelling of God in the Spirit* (Ephesians 2:19-22).

We know that Jesus built His new priesthood upon a foundation of the apostles and prophets, with Himself as the Chief Cornerstone. Jesus embodies all five ascension gifts and brings balance to the structure. In Christ, even in His temperament as the Man from Nazareth, we see the origins of the genius that animates all aspects of the fivefold ministry. His Body is *"the fullness of Him who fills all in all"* (Eph. 1:23). Through Him comes the continual release of genius in every generation *"until we all attain to the unity of the faith, and of the knowledge of the Son of God, to a mature man, to the measure of the stature which belongs to the fullness of Christ"* (Eph. 4:13).

Christ's Finished Work

You cannot build upon the foundation of Christ as Chief Cornerstone unless He has already come, died, passed from death to life, and taken His place at the Father's right hand. The finished work of the cross is the undeniable prerequisite to the building of the new faith community. The finished work includes not only His death on Friday but also His resurrection on Sunday. This is the true preaching of the cross of Jesus Christ.

There is no other message because *"there is salvation in no one else"* (Acts 4:12).

Pinpoint the Prophetic

1. Why was it necessary for John the Baptist to serve as prophet when the One to whom he pointed was clearly visible? How is the oneness of the message and the messenger relevant to the timing of his ministry and Jesus' assessment of John's greatness?

2. Describe the Exodus parallels between the ministries of Moses and John the Baptist. Describe an Exodus moment in your life or your family's life. How was your imagination restructured to produce this event?

3. Describe two stumbling blocks that caused Jewish leaders to deny Jesus' identity as Messiah. How might their leadership positions have contributed to their blindness?

4. Jesus' miracles profoundly affected the Jewish imagination. How do miracles or the lack thereof affect and reflect upon our faith communities today?

5. Practically speaking, how was Moses' ministry fulfilled in Christ?

Chapter 10

Paul: Prophet of Grace and Master Builder

He has said to me, "My grace is sufficient for you, for power is perfected in weakness." Most gladly, therefore, I will rather boast about my weaknesses, that the power of Christ may dwell in me. Therefore I am well content with weaknesses, with insults, with distresses, with persecutions, with difficulties, for Christ's sake; for when I am weak, then I am strong (2 CORINTHIANS 12:9-10).

THE MAN WHO WROTE TWO-THIRDS OF THE NEW TESTAMENT WAS A living testimony of the Gospel of grace, *"a vessel for honor, sanctified, useful to the Master, prepared for every good work"* (2 Tim. 2:21). As a Pharisee and persecutor complicit in the murders of Christ followers, he would seem an unlikely candidate. But in the wisdom of God he was the perfect choice. Saul of Tarsus, better known as the apostle Paul, lived the message of Jesus Christ.

Upon his conversion, the man known for hunting down Christ followers rejoiced to be counted among the hunted. Years later, when he was beaten by a mob in Jerusalem, he did not retreat to recover from his wounds but instead spoke to the Jews who were so offended by his witness. He responded to their brutality, not with anger but with compassion. And he spoke in their language, Hebrew:

> I am a Jew, born in Tarsus of Cilicia, but brought up in this city, educated under Gamaliel, strictly according to the law of our fathers, being zealous for God, just as you all are today. I persecuted this Way to the death, binding and putting both men and women into prisons, as also the high priest and all the Council of the elders can testify (Acts 22:3-5).

Paul went on to share the details of his Damascus Road experience. The crowd was not comforted but became more infuriated and questioned whether Paul had the right to go on living (see Acts 22:22).

From beginning to end, Paul's ministry was charged with controversy. Yet he never declined his mission. He understood his role and the heavenly reward that would follow (see 2 Tim. 4:8). Most of all, Paul understood the transforming power of the cross to the degree that opposition could not deter him. Paul was well-equipped by God for the rigors of his work. If anyone understood the ferocious defense of Jewish tradition, he did. Well-versed in the Law and the prized protégé of the prominent teacher, Gamaliel,[1] Paul was a premier apologist and the youngest man ever to sit on the Sanhedrin.

Then known as Saul, he watched as Stephen was martyred. According to Luke's account, *"Saul was in hearty agreement with putting him to death"* (Acts 8:1). Saul was not satisfied to persecute the Church in Jerusalem. So determined was he to root out the testimony of Christ that he sought to round up His followers in other cities:

> Saul, still breathing threats and murder against the disciples of the Lord, went to the high priest, and asked for letters from him to the synagogues at Damascus, so that if he found any belonging to the Way, both men and women, he might bring them bound to Jerusalem (Acts 9:1-2).

From the beginning it must have seemed to believers of the Way that their annihilation was assured. Opposition was fierce, and natural defenses were limited. Stephen's death unleashed a *"great persecution—against the church in Jerusalem"* (Acts 8:1). But instead of extinguishing the Church, adversity served to spread the Gospel farther as *"they were all scattered throughout the regions of Judea and Samaria, except the apostles"* (Acts 8:1).

Fleeing certain death, followers of Christ carried the Gospel with them. Even the ferocity of Saul's zeal could not prevent the eternal purpose of God. The scattering or *diaspora* of the nascent Church was integral to her growth.

The Damascus Road Encounter

Saul the persecutor was granted authority to comb the city of Damascus for Christians and return them, in bonds, to Jerusalem. He packed up his posse and headed out. But instead of rounding up Christ followers for the slaughter, he was arrested by the Son of God:

> As he was traveling, it happened that as he was approaching Damascus, and suddenly a light from heaven flashed around him; and he fell to the ground, and heard a voice saying to him, **"Saul, Saul, why are you persecuting Me?"** (Acts 9:3-4).

Saul asked aloud, *"Who art You, Lord?' And He said, 'I am Jesus whom you are persecuting'"* (Acts 9:5). On the one hand Saul realized that he was talking to God; on the other, he seemed unsure. According to Paul's account from Acts 26:14 the Lord also said: *"It is hard for you to kick against the goads"*. Adam Clarke explains that kicking against the goads is the habit of stubborn livestock:

> *Kentron* [translated "prick" or "goad"], signifies an ox goad, a piece of pointed iron stuck in the end of a stick, with which the ox is urged on when drawing the plow. The origin of the proverb seems to have been this: sometimes it happens that a restive or stubborn ox kicks back against the goad, and thus wounds himself more deeply....[2]

Jesus' words seem to indicate that Saul had heard His voice in some form before the Damascus Road encounter. Had Jesus spoken to Saul's heart as

Stephen and others perished or as Saul celebrated the Passover or studied the Scriptures? The answer is unknown; we do know that God's plan had been in effect throughout Saul's life.

Even as Saul studied under Gamaliel, the plan of God was underway. Saul was more fluent in the Hebraic mind-set and scholarship than anyone other than his revered teacher. He understood the offense taken by Jews at the name of Jesus. He was familiar with every argument against Jesus as Messiah. For all of his lifetime, God had been grooming Saul. Just as Moses had been educated in the ways of Pharaoh, Saul was thoroughly equipped to address the Jews' trepidation and to speak to the Gentiles, whom God would graft into His eternal vine.

The doma temperament was in place; his unique résumé had already been in development. Though his life was full of seeming contradictions, Saul had been perfectly suited to serve as a New Covenant prophet. The only remaining question would be answered by Saul as he lay sprawled on the hard surface of the Damascus Road.

The ball was in his court.

Saul Responds to Christ

In Acts 9:6, the Lord directed Saul to enter Damascus and await further instructions. Saul responded by obeying God. Years later, before King Agrippa, Paul recounted his testimony, saying, *"I did not prove disobedient to the heavenly vision"* (Acts 26:19). Paul was indeed obedient. But the heavenly vision was not God's plan for Paul's future. It was not even the restoration of his eyesight by Ananias (see Acts 9:17-18). The heavenly vision was the revelation of Christ. It was profound and almost diametrically opposed to everything Saul believed and lived prior to the Damascus Road.

Like Moses at the burning bush, Saul repented: he turned toward the Man in the Glory, Jesus Christ, and was consumed with Him. The elite defender of the Law of Moses became the quintessential prophet of the Lord Jesus Christ and the master builder of His Church (see 1 Cor. 3:10). Completely devoted to God's people and cause, he was entrusted to steward the mystery revealed through the death and resurrection of Jesus Christ:

> *Now I rejoice in my sufferings for your sake, and in my flesh I do my share on behalf of His body* (which is the church) *in filling up that which is lacking in Christ's afflictions. Of this church I was made a minister according to the **stewardship from God bestowed on me for your benefit, that I might fully carry out the preaching of the word of God, that is, the mystery which has been hidden from the past ages and generations;** but has now been manifested to His saints* (Colossians 1:24-26).

Saul's encounter with Christ also revealed the relationship between Him and His Body. Remember, the Lord said: *"I am Jesus whom you are persecuting"* (Acts 9:5). Christ had already ascended; Saul persecuted His followers. But from Jesus' words, Saul inferred the relationship: Christ (the Head) and His Body (the Church) are inseparable. If you persecute the Body, you persecute Christ.

This understanding of Christ and His Church is critical for apostolic and prophetic ministry. Saul obeyed the heavenly vision and was consumed with Christ. Having aligned himself with God's eternal purpose, he served the balance of his life to uphold the connection between Head and Body. This is an aspect of his commitment to God's purpose: the filling of all things described in Ephesians 4:10. Saul's example should guide today's ascension gifts: The degree to which apostles and prophets obey the heavenly vision (Christ Himself) is the degree to which the Church will rise to her full stature.

HEAVENLY VISION OR VISION STATEMENT?

The heavenly vision mentioned by Paul in Acts 26:19 is not a vision for destiny or a vision statement. The heavenly vision is Jesus Christ, the Man in the Glory. Those who are obedient to the vision find their lives and purpose in Him.

Prophet in Process

Paul's awareness of his calling paralleled Jeremiah's (see Jer. 1:5). Both men came to realize, in the course of their ministries, that they had been called by God from the womb: Paul wrote: *"He who had set me apart, even from my mother's womb...called me through His grace..."* (Gal. 1:15).

At some point the divergent epochs in Paul's life were fused in one, as Galatians 1:15 attests. Having applied his unique qualifications in the fulfillment of his calling, Paul realized that his past was no mistake. In his letter to the Galatians, for example, his deep knowledge of Judaism positioned him to address the confusion over circumcision and Christian adherence to the Law. Over the course of his ministry, Paul's expert exegetical skills dovetailed perfectly with his prophetic gifting to provide the Church with a strong doctrinal footing.

Although Saul had been set apart from the womb, he would need to be set apart for a season of process after his encounter with Jesus. Not that Saul was shy about his calling; within days of his conversion, he began preaching in Damascus:

> *Immediately he began to proclaim Jesus in the synagogues, saying, "He is the Son of God." And all those hearing him continued to be amazed, and were saying, "Is this not he who in Jerusalem destroyed those who called on this name, and who had come here for the purpose of bringing them bound before the chief priests?"* (Acts 9:20-21).

It was inevitable that Saul would ruffle religious feathers:

> ...[he confounded] *the Jews who lived at Damascus by proving that this Jesus is the Christ. And when many days had elapsed,* **the Jews plotted together to do away with him,** *but their plot became known to Saul....his disciples took him by night, and let him down through an opening in the wall, lowering him in a large basket* (Acts 9:22-25).

After fleeing into the Arabian wilderness, Saul remained isolated for 14 years. As persona non grata among the Jews in Jerusalem, he visited there only briefly to meet Peter and James (see Gal. 1:18-19). He then spent a decade ministering in his hometown of Tarsus. During Saul's exile and before he assumed a recognized leadership role, the Church continued to grow; the Gentile church at Antioch was established; and Philip ignited revival in Samaria.

PHILIP IN SAMARIA

Persecution drove Philip into Samaria, where he was enormously successful in spreading the Gospel. His evangelistic gift and anointed preaching won many souls and drove out demons (see Acts 8:4-12). *"Now when the apostles in Jerusalem heard that Samaria had received the word of God, they sent them Peter and John"* (Acts 8:14). Philip's ministry birthed converts, but he needed the apostles Peter and John to establish a church for them and for future followers of Christ. Once these governmental leaders arrived, Philip departed from Samaria and encountered the Ethiopian eunuch (see Acts 8:27-29), in effect sowing the Word of God in yet another nation.

Saul in Exile

Saul's period of isolation was no mistake. It was a season of purpose, process, and development from which he would emerge with a revelation that came, not from mentors and established leaders, but directly from the Holy Spirit. Fourteen years set apart from the standard bearers of the faith had served to make Saul absolutely confident of his revelation and role in the plan of God.

During his exile, Saul discovered the mystery of Christ living in us and the us living in Christ. We can easily take his revelation for granted because we are familiar with the truths expressed in his letters. But what he was directed to share was revolutionary—and really, still is. The truth of *"Christ in you, the hope of glory"* (Col. 1:27) and the reality of being *"in Christ Jesus"*

(Rom. 8:1) are life-altering. The ramifications to individuals, the Church, and the world cannot be overstated.

The confidence of Saul's personal relationship with Christ was a key component of his effectiveness. While he regarded *"James and Cephas and John, who were reputed to be pillars..."* (Gal. 2:9), he was not intimidated by their having preceded him in the faith; nor was he hindered by his former reputation as their persecutor (although some distrusted him at first). Instead, Paul wrote as one chosen by God, just as they had been chosen:

> From those who were of high reputation (what they were makes no difference to me; God shows no partiality)—well, those who were of reputation contributed nothing to me. But on the contrary, seeing that I had been entrusted with the gospel to the uncircumcised, just as Peter had been to the circumcised (for He who effectually worked for Peter in his apostleship to the circumcised effectually worked for me also to the Gentiles) (Galatians 2:6-8).

Saul suffered persecution during his exile. His father was a rabbi who was, no doubt, as zealous for the Law as Saul had been. When Paul returned to Tarsus after his conversion, he would certainly have faced demands to renounce Christ. In addition, as a Pharisee, Saul was necessarily married and would be subsequently divorced by his wife on the grounds of his heresy. It is also believed that some of the hardships (including scourging) described in Second Corinthians 11 occurred during Saul's 14-year isolation. He endured the process of prophetic maturation until his own body bore the marks of Christ.

Paul the Miracle-Worker

We know that the New Covenant offices of prophet and apostle are closely aligned in terms of their gift mixes. Prophets move in the obvious prophetic gifts of prophecy, the word of wisdom, and the word of knowledge, but also in the discerning of spirits, the gift of faith, and the working of miracles, as apostles do.

Saul's ministry began in the prophetic and progressed into the apostolic when he and Barnabas were commissioned by command of the Holy Spirit (see Acts 13:2). Always, Saul's ministry was marked by signs and wonders, as he himself attested: *"The signs of a true apostle were performed among you with all perseverance, by signs and wonders and miracles"* (2 Cor. 12:12). In Acts 13, Saul's dealings with the false prophet Bar-Jesus resulted in the latter's temporary blindness. In Acts 14:10, he ministered healing to a man lame from birth. In Ephesus, *"God was performing extraordinary miracles by the hands of Paul, so that handkerchiefs or aprons were even carried from his body to the sick, and the diseases left them and the evil spirits went out"* (Acts 19:11-12). He raised a young man, Eutychus, from the dead after he had fallen from a window during the apostle's preaching (see Acts 20:9-10).

Like Moses, whose ministry was marked by signs and wonders, and Jesus, who was the most profound of miracle workers, Paul exemplified the qualities of the prophet and apostle in the working of miracles.

PAUL AND THE CHARISMATA

Paul's teaching on the nine gifts in First Corinthians 12:8-10 implies that he operated in all of them:

1. Word of wisdom	2. Word of knowledge	3. Faith
4. Gifts of healing	5. Miracles	6. Prophecy
7. Discerning of spirits	8. Tongues	9. Interpretation of tongues

Paul at Antioch

There is no economy more exquisite than God's! By it, Saul's persecution would scatter Christians to Antioch, and God would in turn send Saul there to help establish the church on a firm footing:

*So then those who were scattered because of the persecution that arose in connection with Stephen made their way to Phoenicia and Cyprus and Antioch, **speaking the word to no one except to Jews alone*** (Acts 11:19).

*But there were some of them, men of Cyprus and Cyrene, who came to Antioch **and began speaking to the Greeks also, preaching the Lord Jesus*** (Acts 11:20).

As we have learned, the first eight years of the Church saw outreach almost exclusively to Jews, as Acts 11:19 testifies. Eventually, however, the apostles embraced ministry to the Gentiles. This was the specific ministry to which Saul had been commissioned.

Taken Off the Shelf

Remember that, after he fled Damascus, Saul returned to Tarsus. Meanwhile, the church at Antioch grew and Barnabas was sent to them: *"The news about* [the believers] *reached the ears of the church at Jerusalem, and they sent Barnabas off to Antioch"* (Acts 11:22). Barnabas, known as "the son of consolation" (see Acts 4:36), was likely sent by those in Jerusalem who still had little interest in reaching the Gentiles. He went and was moved by what he saw but realized the lack of spiritual leadership and government. He encouraged the people to keep the faith and added many new believers to their numbers. Then Barnabas left Antioch in search of help:

He left for Tarsus to look for Saul; and when he had found him, he brought him to Antioch. And for an entire year they met with the church and taught considerable numbers; and the disciples were first called Christians in Antioch (Acts 11:25-26).

Barnabas' and Saul's paths had crossed a dozen years earlier. In fact, Barnabas had vouched for Saul when believers in Jerusalem feared and distrusted him, no doubt because of his past brutalization of them:

When he [Saul] *had come to Jerusalem, he was trying to associate with the disciples; and they were all afraid of him, not believing that he was a disciple. But Barnabas took hold of him and brought him to the apostles and described to them how he had seen the Lord on the road, and that He had talked to him, and how at Damascus he had spoken out boldly in the name of Jesus* (Acts 9:26-27).

Finding Saul was most likely difficult. Barnabas could more easily have recruited a leader from Jerusalem. In God's wisdom, this was not to be. Peter was certainly not ready for the assignment. Although God had already addressed his bias against Gentiles (see Acts 10), Peter continued to favor Jewish believers, as Paul revealed in his letter to the Galatians:

> *But when Cephas came to Antioch, I opposed him to his face.... For prior to the coming of certain men from James, he used to eat with the Gentiles; but when they came, he began to withdraw and hold himself aloof, fearing the party of the circumcision. The rest of the Jews joined him in hypocrisy, with the result that even Barnabas was carried away by their hypocrisy* (Galatians 2:11-13).

Saul confronted Peter in a public and authoritative way. He asked a question that cut to the core of Peter's hypocrisy: *"If you, being a Jew, live like the Gentiles and not like the Jews, how is it that you compel the Gentiles to live like Jews?"* (Gal. 2:14). Peter never had been the man for Antioch; Saul was, and by the Spirit of God, Barnabas knew that. He remembered Saul's fervency and knew that Saul had been "on the shelf" for some time. He also knew that Saul had suffered rejection from traditional Jews and from followers of Christ. Now, the season of rejection and exile had served its purpose; it was time for Saul to be on the Church's frontlines.

Now, the season of rejection and exile had served its purpose; it was time for Saul to be on the Church's frontlines.

Saul Begins Building

When he arrived at Antioch, Saul was not yet commissioned as an apostle. However, he operated out of more than a revelatory prophetic gift and was able, with Barnabas, to set the church in much-needed order. This is where the strong connection between the prophetic and apostolic is readily apparent. Although Saul flowed in his prophetic anointing, he also functioned in a structural, foundational, governmental gift. It was apparent that Saul was gifted for the apostolic and possessed the wisdom to build wisely. This is what Antioch needed—a man focused on building the Church.

If you remember our comparison of the fivefold ministry to a human hand, the apostle is the thumb that must touch all other gifts to perform his or her function. Saul and Barnabas began as prophet-teachers in Antioch but were in process in the other offices. For example, during Barnabas' first trip to Antioch *"considerable numbers were brought to the Lord"* (Acts 11:24). Both he and Saul grew in their gifts so that by the time Saul was released into apostolic ministry at Antioch, he had functioned in all five offices. With his broad experience, Saul was qualified to counsel others (see Acts 20:28; 2 Tim. 4:5).

SAUL, THE EVANGELIST

During his exile from Jerusalem, Saul remained fervent in ministry and preached the Gospel in Damascus. Upon his return to Tarsus he was "actively engaged in evangelizing the Gentiles."[3] That is where Barnabas found and recruited Saul for the mission at Antioch.

From Prophet to Apostle

In Antioch, Saul found an ethnically diverse body of believers and a limited group of leaders. Among the prophets and teachers who served with Saul and Barnabas were *"Simeon who was called Niger, and Lucius of Cyrene, and Manaen who had been brought up with Herod the tetrarch..."* (Acts 13:1). Simeon is believed by many Bible scholars to be Simon of Cyrene, the man who carried Jesus' cross (see Luke 23:26). Simeon and the others were helping the saints at Antioch and serving in some semblance of leadership roles.

At this point, Antioch was being served by five prophet-teachers but lacked apostolic leadership. From the beginning, Jerusalem, where the

Church began, had 12 apostles. Do you see the progression from apostles to prophets? It is the same order Paul wrote about in First Corinthians 12:28: *"God has appointed in the church, **first apostles, second prophets, third teachers,** then miracles, then gifts of healings, helps, administrations, various kinds of tongues."* Jerusalem had apostolic leadership; Antioch had only prophet-teachers in their ranks.

This soon changed, as Acts 13:2 reveals: *"While they were ministering to the Lord and fasting, the Holy Spirit said, **'Set apart for Me Barnabas and Saul for the work to which I have called them.'"** As the prophets and teachers fasted and prayed, a word came from the Holy Spirit and all of them bore witness to it. This is the first biblical example of the laying on of hands by the presbytery in the New Covenant Church (see Paul's later reference in First Timothy 4:14).

At that moment, Saul and Barnabas, who were known as prophets and teachers, were commissioned as apostles. This established awareness within the Gentile church at Antioch of a pattern by which apostles would emerge from those who had a prophetic teaching gift. It is important to note that not all prophets and teachers are apostles; however some (based on the measure and range of giftings) eventually enter an apostolic measure of rule.

Q. Are apostles church-planters?

A. Building churches is part of the apostolic measure of rule. Apostles also steward the mystery of Christ in us. It is a clear central message when they speak. There is a third aspect of the apostolic that must be mentioned: apostles reproduce themselves, in terms of leadership function. They are not lone rangers perched atop the fivefold "ladder." Just as Paul had a team, modern-day apostles work with others and mentor them, thereby ensuring continuity in the future.

The Wise Master Builder

We are God's fellow workers; you are God's field, God's build-ing. **According to the grace of God which was given to me, like a wise master builder** *I laid a foundation, and another is building upon it. But each man must be careful how he builds upon it. For no man can lay a foundation other than the one which is laid, which is Jesus Christ* (1 Corinthians 3:9-11).

Paul the apostle testified of the grace he had been given to build the Church of Jesus Christ. Having participated in all aspects of the fivefold ministry, he was indeed a master builder whose legacy among prophets and apostles is rivaled only by that of Jesus Christ.

In keeping with the truth that the prophet is the message, even Paul's occupation as a tentmaker (see Acts 18:1-2) spoke of his Kingdom assign-ment—*building*. (Interestingly, the Prophet and Sent One was also a builder in the natural sense: He was a carpenter!) Paul's mastery of building was based in his motivation: the intent of God to raise not only converts but churches. Perhaps Paul's greatest achievement in this regard was the church at Ephesus.

When Paul arrived there, he rented quarters from a Greek mystery school (what we would call "New Age Headquarters"). For two years he focused his teaching on Jesus of Nazareth and the resurrection from the dead. So impactful was his message that in two years' time 40,000 came to Christ and became part of the Ephesian church.

The work was not accomplished singlehandedly. Paul traveled with a team of between 14 and 70 people. His team method of ministry ensured the fulfillment of his calling and empowered his helpers to pursue their callings. It also afforded new churches the opportunity to be firmly established and therefore effective. In Ephesus, for example, all aspects of the fivefold minis-try were in operation. Ephesus was a thriving, active church—an example to churches everywhere. Sadly this vibrant church slipped into decline. Within 25 years of Paul's death, the overall Church was in a diminished state, as five of Jesus' seven letters to the churches reveal (see Rev. 2–3).

BE ON GUARD

Paul's epistles to the churches at Colossae and Ephesus reflect the highest revelations of the Church of Jesus Christ in all of Scripture. Yet, no church is immune to decay, and even the strongest churches must be vigilant to remain fruitful. In their glory days, Paul prophesied a falling away to his beloved Ephesians:

Be on guard for yourselves and for all the flock.... I know that after my departure savage wolves will come in among you, not sparing the flock (Acts 20:28-29).

Revelation 2:4 records the fulfillment of Paul's prophecy: "*But I have this against you* [Ephesus], *that you have left your first love.*"

Paul's ministry was essential to the building of the Church of Jesus Christ. Although the Body has experienced ebbs and flows, Paul's work was never in vain. The Church continues to be mentored by Paul's teaching. The wise master builder contributed to the establishment of an undeniable and lasting heritage—and continues to prepare the Bride for the Bridegroom's return!

Pinpoint the Prophetic

1. How do the ironies of Paul's life story encourage you? How do they change your thinking or shed light on aspects of your calling?

2. Just as the persecution of the early Church caused suffering and raised doubts, modern-day events give us pause. Compare and contrast the difficulties faced by the Church in the 1st and 21st centuries. What do your observations reveal?

3. Antioch was a turning point in Saul's ministry. How does his process inform yours? What specific lessons apply? Explain.

4. Do you have a Barnabas? How has he or she helped facilitate the plan of God in your life? If no such figure is yet seen, how might God's timing be in play?

5. What is the condition of your church, spiritually speaking? What is your role? Has a change in leadership affected the spiritual climate? Explain.

Chapter 11

The Church, the Spirit, and the Anointing

And likewise, all the prophets who have spoken, from Samuel and his successors onward, also announced these days. "It is you who are the sons of the prophets and of the covenant which God made with your fathers, saying to Abraham, 'And in your seed all the families of the earth shall be blessed'" (ACTS 3:24-25).

ON THE DAY OF PENTECOST, 120 BECAME 3,000 AS THE DIVINE nature was infused throughout those who confessed Christ. During just the first few years in Jerusalem alone, tens of thousands became followers of the Way. Jesus' called-out company has multiplied from that day to this.

The Church was built upon the revelation of Jesus Christ and a new relationship with the Holy Spirit. The fledgling community had begun to coalesce in the days of John the Baptist and continued to grow under the earthly ministry of the Messiah. But the Church became fully operational only after the ascension of the Savior. This was in keeping with His promise regarding Holy Spirit: *"But I tell you the truth, it is to your advantage that*

I go away; for if I do not go away, the Helper will not come to you; but if I go, I will send Him to you" (John 16:7).

After the ascension and through the ministry of the Holy Spirit, the Church became God's new prophetic instrument in the earth. The prophetic was not new; true prophets ministered under the Old Covenant and announced God's eternal purpose to people and nations. But this new prophetic instrument was the embodiment of the Son of God—literally the Body of Christ—and would proclaim Him from the ascension onward.

Do you remember Moses' prophecy about the Prophet, Jesus Christ? (See Deuteronomy 18:15.) The prophecy became a touchstone for Jews, but no sooner was it uttered than it was followed by a warning from the Lord:

> *I will raise up for them a Prophet like you from among their brethren, and will put My words in His mouth, and He shall speak to them all that I command Him.* ***And it shall be that whoever will not hear My words, which He speaks in My name, I will require it of him*** (Deuteronomy 18:18-20 NKJV).

Long before Christ came in the flesh, God prepped His people with the wisdom to receive Him. Peter restated the ancient warning: *"Every soul that does not heed that prophet shall be utterly destroyed from among the people'"* (Acts 3:23) and demonstrated continuity of the revelation by placing it in the context of prophetic history. He stressed this continuity by reminding his listeners of their identity as *"the sons of the prophets, and of the covenant which God made with your fathers, saying to Abraham, 'And in your seed all the families of the earth shall be blessed'"* (Acts 3:25).

The finished work of Christ, the words of Moses, and the blessing of Abraham fall under a single rubric: the unfolding of God's eternal purpose. The significance of the continuum is evident in the language of God's warning: *"Every soul"* that fails to heed the Prophet will be *"utterly destroyed."* The adverb *utterly* was not used to increase the Bible's word count. It is a point of emphasis that should stir and motivate us—utterly—to confront error, false doctrine, complacency, human ideologies, and any *isms* that are not *"captive to the obedience of Christ"* (2 Cor. 10:5).

Our mandate regarding the testimony of Jesus is clear:

Speaking the truth in love, we are to grow up in all aspects into Him, who is the head, even Christ, from whom the whole body, being fitted and held together by that which every joint supplies, according to the proper working of each individual part, causes the growth of the body for the building up of itself in love (Ephesians 4:15-16).

The ascension did more than resolve the death, burial, and resurrection of Christ. It became the cosmic trigger point that released the Church to transact Kingdom "business" in the earth. In addition, it inaugurated the building up of the Body by *"that which every joint supplies."*

The Local Expression of King and Kingdom

The Church and the Kingdom are inseparable and inextricably linked in the unfolding of God's eternal purpose. Those who declare the end of the Church age and the beginning of the Kingdom era bear the weight of tortured arguments to support their case. God's plan is more elegant than that: the Body of Christ exists to express the testimony of its Head, the King of kings (and by extension, His Kingdom). In the simplest (and perhaps most profound) of terms, churches are local expressions of the Kingdom message and all it implies. Each church is unique yet conveys larger truths that are held in common. Paul captured the interconnectedness of churches through a variety of metaphors and descriptions:

*I write so that you may know how one ought to conduct himself in **the household of God,** which is the church of the living God, the pillar and support of the truth* (1 Timothy 3:15).

*Be on guard for yourselves and for all the flock, among which the Holy Spirit has made you overseers, to shepherd **the church of God** which He purchased with His own blood* (Acts 20:28).

*And might reconcile them both in **one body** to God through the cross, by it having put to death the enmity* (Ephesians 2:16).

Paul also spoke of Christ followers as soldiers; therefore the Church is, metaphorically speaking, the army of God in the earth.

> *Who at any time serves as **a soldier** at his own expense? Who plants a vineyard, and does not eat the fruit of it? Or who tends a flock and does not use the milk of the flock?* (1 Corinthians 9:7)

> *But I thought it necessary to send to you Epaphroditus, my brother and fellow worker and **fellow soldier**, who is also your messenger and minister to my need* (Philippians 2:25).

> *Suffer hardship with me, as **a good soldier** of Christ Jesus. No **soldier** in active service entangles himself in the affairs of everyday life, so that he may please the one who enlisted him as **a soldier*** (2 Timothy 2:3-4).

Remember what undergirds the Body of Christ: it is the specific foundation of apostles and prophets. Remember also what holds the building together: He is the Chief Cornerstone, Jesus Christ (see Eph. 2:20). When Paul referred to these apostles and prophets, he was speaking of the apostolic and prophetic offices. A local church will typically have numerous prophetically-motivated people; but a sound foundation will include apostles and true prophets who will serve together to build and ensure the health of the building.

THE HOUSEHOLD OF GOD	THE CHURCH OF GOD	THE BODY OF CHRIST	THE ARMY OF GOD

Functional or Faking It?

For the healthy expression of the Kingdom to be demonstrated through earthen vessels and local churches, there must be a commitment to spiritual soundness. Just as it true of personal health, marital health, and financial well-being, the church's condition must be monitored. Unless there is frankness and objectivity about the way things are and a commitment to how they ought to be, functionality is impaired.

It does little good to establish a hierarchy and ignore the fundamentals of church health. Remember that *apostle, prophet, evangelist, pastor, and teacher* are not titles but functions. The ascension gifts are *all about* function. The local church can do all the "right" things—hold board meetings, cast the vision, baptize converts, care for the broken, feed the hungry—but unless these works spring from the heavenly vision and the transforming work of the cross, these works are irrelevant. Transformation must be the goal and always by way of the anointing—that is, the Holy Spirit.

Jesus' letters to the seven churches of Asia Minor (see Rev. 2–3) were honest assessments of spiritual condition. The five corrective letters were not designed to demoralize or negate; they were instructive and meant to redeem shortfalls. Likewise, the two laudatory letters were not pats on the back or invitations to maintain the status quo; they helped churches to know where they were hitting the mark and to what they should aspire.

From the beginning of this book, we have taken an honest look at the modern Church and at the hallmarks that reveal our current condition. We talked about the lack of critical thinking and the corresponding theological and spiritual shallowness that accepts whatever is shared, preached, or proclaimed as being truth. Too often, the Gospel is spoon-fed in predigested formulas; the teaching and other forms of ministry are functional enough to keep believers hanging on but not enough to produce spiritually stable disciples. Many float from church to church in search of "a word" or a "new" revelation or a social experience. Transformation not only seems out of reach, but it becomes inconvenient.

The place of transformation is rarely comfortable. Those who are grounded in truth and focused on the heavenly vision will submit to the process. Those who are accustomed to sermonettes and seeker-friendly attractions will find it difficult to commit and will often forfeit the transformation they desire. A strong foundation in the apostolic and prophetic is needed to align churches with His eternal purpose and rewire the imagination of the local body.

WHOSE MESSAGE IS IT?

Too easily, the Church falls under the sway of titles. Assuming the existence of the Ephesians 2:20 foundation of apostles and prophets, we should be asking questions. What message is the apostle attempting to steward? Is it the mystery of Christ in us or a message not germane to the apostle's measure of rule? Is the prophet testifying of Christ or prophesying outside the "river banks" of His intent? Are we attracted by the anointing of the Holy Spirit or dazzled by a gift? Have we come into agreement with a fallacy? Or have we measured every word against the standard of Scripture? It behooves us to follow John's advice: *"Beloved, do not believe every spirit, but test the spirits to see whether they are from God, because many false prophets have gone out into the world"* (1 John 4:1).

Belief in Christ is not a passive act; it is a hands-on enterprise. While salvation is received in a moment of time, living for Christ involves a continuum of decisions made not as works of the flesh but by way of the Holy Spirit. The same is true of the local church: all it is and does must flow from its reliance upon the Holy Spirit. Only then are we free to acknowledge our strengths and weaknesses, embrace correction, and resist compromise.

Paul's prayer for the church at Ephesus is apt:

> *That He would grant you, according to the riches of His glory, to be strengthened with power through His Spirit in the inner man; so that Christ may dwell in your hearts through faith; and that you, being rooted and grounded in love, may be able to comprehend with all the saints what is the breadth and length and height and depth, and to know the love of Christ which surpasses knowledge,* ***that you may be filled up to all the fullness of God*** *(Ephesians 3:16-19).*

New Apostolic Reformation

The pressing need in this hour is for a new apostolic reformation. In His intent to fill all things in Christ, the foundation of apostles and prophets must be strong. In some quarters, such a foundation has not existed for centuries; in others, the foundation is in need of repairs. It is not surprising that, all over the world, conferences are being held on this very topic. The attention being paid the issue is laudable, but we must be certain that we are pursuing God's intent and not trafficking in terminology.

This warning is strident and warranted. Two thousand years after the Day of Pentecost, we have flourished in some areas and ceded territory in others. The tendency to recycle Charismatic concepts is counterproductive at best and toxic at worst. In order to ensure a sound foundation built on the apostles and prophets, we must be determined to establish balance in the Church—doctrinal balance, structural balance, and a sound balance of ascension gifts.

Of great concern is the development of churches that rest not on sound government but on a secularized independent spirit. We claim to desire the true government of Almighty God, but too often we contribute (because we lack clear borders, sound structures, and the mettle to risk offending others) to a Charismatic free-for-all in which parking lot prophecies and off-the-cuff declarations tickle our ears and draw us off course, individually and corporately.

This is *not* what is meant by a new apostolic reformation. In fact, there is nothing new about it. It is, metaphorically, a river without banks—in other words, *a flood*. Do you remember Ezekiel's vision of the river flowing from the Temple? The river signified life; the water got deeper and deeper until the prophet could not touch bottom. As nourishing as the water was, the Lord brought Ezekiel back to its banks, which were lined with fruit trees that yielded food and healing (see Ezek. 47).

Although we pursue the deep waters of revelation and spiritual growth, we must also value the river banks that keep our waters flowing in beneficial ways. The Church functions best when her government is balanced, able to ensure the unhindered flow of grace and the steady growth of the "sheep."

REFORMATION REALITIES

Where there is reformation, transformation is evident. It is the striking degree of change that lifts the saints and the Church out of dead traditions, complacency, and error. It inspires a return to a superior condition or position and recovers the testimony of Christ. In the absence of this striking degree of change, what is labeled *reformation* may be little more than *renovation*. True reformation will always and must always bear recognizable and lasting fruit.

Principles and Anointing

In order to remain attuned to God's enduring principles, apostles and prophets must always operate under the anointing of the Holy Spirit. In all areas of spiritual pursuit, they must function in the grace and knowledge of God rather than in their human ability or understanding.

When Zerubbabel was called to complete the Temple, the Jews had little power and few resources. The task must have seemed overwhelming. The prophet came with a much-needed word of encouragement and reminded Zerubbabel that the Lord's ability and unfailing provision would determine the outcome:

> *Not by might nor by power, but by My Spirit...What are you, O great mountain? Before Zerubbabel you will become a plain; and he will bring forth the top stone with shouts of "Grace, grace to it!"* (Zechariah 4:6-7).

There are three ways we can attempt to do the work of God: we can trust our own strength and wisdom; we can borrow the resources of the world: or we can depend on the power of God. The first two approaches may appear to succeed, but they'll fail in the end. Only work done through the power of the Spirit will glorify God and endure the fires of His judgment (see 1 Cor. 3:12-15).[1]

Everything we build will be tested—in an open-book test. God never changes or deviates from His fixed principles and He faithfully reveals His intent through them. Foremost among these principles is Paul's description of Christ's position: *"If then you have been raised up with Christ, keep seeking the things above, where Christ is, seated at the right hand of God"* (Col. 3:1). All that we are called to do and be is based in the reality that He died, was resurrected, and is now seated at the Father's right hand.

> *Everything we build will be tested—in an open-book test.*
> *God never changes or deviates from His fixed principles.*

For God's intent to be fulfilled, the Church must adhere to this principle and be found in Christ who is in high places. This is the most important reason for apostles and prophets to move in their gifts because it is the essential element of the testimony of Jesus. Were He not seated at the Father's right hand, the work of the cross would be incomplete and the corresponding promises would be empty.

But Jesus said, *"I go and prepare a place for you...I will come again, and receive you to Myself, that where I am, there you may be also"* (John 14:2-3). This is more about our placement in the Body of Christ than it is about a mansion in glory. Here is my paraphrase of Jesus' words:

> As The Lamb, I am going beyond the veil and into the Holy of Holies where only the high priest could go once each year. You tied a rope around his ankle before he entered in, so that if he breathed his last in My Presence, you could pull him out. My entry beyond the veil is different. I am going to sprinkle My own blood on the altar, and I will never perish. This High Priest will not be pulled out on a rope. Instead, I will pull you into Myself so that *"where I am, there you may be also."*

188 THE **PROPHETIC** PERSPECTIVE

Jesus knew His followers would receive and rely upon the Holy Spirit after His departure. After His resurrection, He *"breathed on them, and said to them, 'Receive the Holy Spirit'"* (John 20:22). Forty-nine days later, the Spirit fell upon 120 in the Upper Room, and they were in essence caught up with Christ in heavenly places (see Eph. 2:6). This was not accomplished through their deaths, rapture, or some miracle of translation. It occurred through the anointing of the Holy Spirit.

Jesus said, *"When He, the Spirit of truth, comes, He will guide you into all the truth..."* (John 16:13). On one level, the anointing illuminates God's principles and causes our vision to align with His. The anointing is also essential for revelation, which is critical to the function of apostles and prophets. Unless these doma gifts rest on the bedrock of divine revelation, the foundation of the Church will necessarily decay.

Revelation is absolutely vital, but let's be clear: revelation is not a "new" understanding discovered outside the banks of the written Word of God. Instead, revelation is the divine exposure of what has been written already but not yet apprehended. The anointing of the Holy Spirit supports our progressive understanding of what God has already prepared for us. Paul explained it this way: *"Eye has not seen, nor ear heard, nor have entered into the heart of man the things which God has prepared for those who love Him"* (1 Cor. 2:9 NKJV).

The anointing is necessary because only the Holy Spirit knows the details of God's eternal plan and purpose. Without the anointing of the Spirit, it is impossible for the apostle or prophet to gaze into those details. Even with the Holy Spirit, we see only in part (see 1 Cor. 13:9). Nevertheless, that part is essential. *"For to us God revealed them* [the things God has prepared for us] *through the Spirit; for the Spirit searches all things, even the depths of God. For who among men knows the thoughts of a man except the spirit of the man, which is in him? Even so the thoughts of God no one knows except the Spirit of God"* (1 Cor. 2:10-11).

The Authentic Anointing

The anointing is the sole property of the Spirit of God and cannot be imitated, duplicated, or delegated by human decree. You can invite believers to attend a class on the prophetic, but you cannot legitimately promise them the anointing to prophesy. When the course is completed and the certificate is signed, the delegation of the anointing is still God's domain.

Consider the succession from Elijah to Elisha. The former had mentored the latter and was about to be taken up by God. Both men knew what was coming. Elijah knew time was short and initiated a conversation about the imminent transition:

> *Elijah said to Elisha, "Ask what I shall do for you before I am taken from you." And Elisha said, "Please, let a double portion of your spirit be upon me." And he said, "You have asked a hard thing...."* (2 Kings 2:9-10).

Elijah knew the anointing came by succession and could not be duplicated by him. Therefore, he could not guarantee the fulfillment of Elisha's request. After all, God had already rejected as candidates the men from Elijah's schools of the prophets in Gilgal, Bethel, and Jericho. If duplication were the process by which the anointing would continue, Elijah's successor could have been selected from their ranks. Instead, God said, *"Elisha the son of Shaphat of Abel-meholah you shall anoint as prophet in your place"* (1 Kings 19:16).

Elijah had God's word as to his successor, and still the prophet answered Elisha's request with a caveat. He understood the dangers of a misstatement or misunderstanding of God's plan for succession. We need to understand this, too. Only the authentic anointing of the Holy Spirit can accomplish His will. This is not to deny all value to courses and seminars. However, if you register in the expectation that someone will lay hands on you and impart a double-portion anointing, you are deceived. The danger of the deception is significant; you might very well receive something, but it might not be the anointing of God—and it could be a spirit of divination. Unless you are alert and operating within God's principles, you might think you are hearing from God when you are in fact hearing from demonic spirits.

The Balanced Body

The Body of Christ, like any other body, functions best when balanced. If the Church was birthed to embody the message of Jesus Christ, then the Holy Spirit must guide her. This is the ultimate balance. To the extent that the Church relies on other sources, she and her people will be compromised and the filling of all things in Christ will remain more of an idea than a reality.

As a wise master builder, Paul had keen insight into God's eternal purpose for His Church and the dangers of building by any methods but His:

> *According to the grace of God which was given to me, like a wise master builder I laid a foundation, and another is building upon it. But let each man be careful how he builds upon it. For no man can lay a foundation other than the one which is laid, which is Jesus Christ. Now if any man builds upon the foundation with gold, silver, precious stones, wood, hay, straw, each man's work will become evident;...because it is to be revealed with fire; and the fire itself will test the quality of each man's work. If any man's work which he has built upon it remains, he will receive a reward. If any man's work is burned up, he will suffer loss; but he himself will be saved, yet so as through fire* (1 Corinthians 3:10-15).

Balance begins with the right foundation (Jesus Christ) and the right materials (those that have eternal rather than temporal value). Balance is maintained when our perspective is not worldly but heavenly. So, as we operate in our gifts and callings, we do so *"decently and in order"* (1 Cor. 14:40 NKJV), with an eye toward God's intent rather than our advancement. While we eagerly embrace the liberty purchased at the cross, we balance it with reverence for the Lordship of the One who *"is before all things, and in* [whom] *all things hold together"* (Col. 1:17). And as we pursue the ultimate goal of God's glory being manifested in the earth, we are not led by signs and wonders but by the Author of them. We submit to His principles, knowing that without godly government, there is no glory.

God is preparing His prophetic instrument in the earth. As John wrote seven times in the Book of Revelation: *"He who has an ear, let him hear what the Spirit says to the churches"* (Rev. 2:7,11,17,29; 3:6,13,22).

Pinpoint the Prophetic

1. Explain in your own words what it means to be the sons of the prophets and of the covenant. What blessings stem from this identity? What responsibilities accrue to us? Consider your church: To what extent are these blessings and responsibilities understood? Explain.

2. How should shortfalls in the Church be handled? How do traditions, doctrine, and the overall health of a particular church affect that body's ability to address and correct shortfalls?

3. What is the role of the anointing in the Church, especially as it relates to apostles and prophets—in terms of illumination? Revelation? How can we test revelation?

4. Keeping in mind Elijah's response to Elisha's request for the double-portion anointing, was Elisha wrong to make such a request? Why or why not?

5. Reread First Corinthians 3:10-15. What does it mean to build upon the foundation with gold, silver, precious stones, wood, hay, and straw? Why are these building materials unsuitable?

Chapter 12

Our Upward Call

*Until we all attain to the unity of the faith, and
of the knowledge of the Son of God, to a mature
man, to the measure of the stature which belongs
to the fullness of Christ* (EPHESIANS 4:13).

PAUL UNDERSTOOD GOD'S INTENT FOR HIS CHURCH AND THERE-
fore, His Kingdom. Paul also understood his place in the process and said, *"I
press on toward the goal for the prize of the upward call of God in Christ Jesus"*
(Phil. 3:14). This is the nature of the call of Christ: it is an upward call to
consciously occupy the seats He assigned when He *"raised us up with Him,
and seated us with Him in the heavenly places in Christ Jesus"* (Eph. 2:6). The
call is given to us individually and as a Body—God's prophetic instrument
in the earth.

When we started this journey through the realm of the prophetic,
we affirmed the central truth that *all Scripture is prophecy*. We traced
the connections between Old and New Covenants and learned how they
unfurl God's eternal purpose in perfect harmony. We have seen that all of
Scripture—from the poetic books to the dietary laws, from Genesis to Revelation—reveals God's unrelenting love and redemptive aim. Through the
millennia, His upward call has been steadfast; from the first Adam to the

Second Adam and beyond, God has led us to Himself and toward *"the full-ness of Christ"* (Eph. 4:13).

During our walk through God's indivisible will, Word, and purpose, we have glimpsed the symmetry of the Torah, the Prophets, and the Wisdom Literature, and their counterparts: the Gospels, the Book of Revelation, and the Epistles. We have mined their truths, particularly from the perspective of the prophetic, and learned who we are and where we came from. Now, it is time to gaze into where we are going.

The Council of the Lord

To view the prophetic in the context of our upward calling and heavenly position in Christ Jesus, we begin with a passage from the Old Testament. Given in rebuke long ago, it is instructive today, both for its caution and insight into prophetic workings. It reveals the divine setting from which prophets have been called and commissioned by God:

> *But who has stood in **the council of the Lord**, that he should see and hear His word? Who has given heed to His word and listened? Behold, the storm of the Lord has gone forth in wrath, even a whirling tempest; it will swirl down on the head of the wicked. The anger of the Lord will not turn back until He has performed and carried out the purposes of His heart; in the last days you will clearly understand it. I did not send these prophets, but they ran. I did not speak to them, but they prophesied. But if they had stood in My council, then they would have announced My words to My people, and would have turned them back from their evil way and from the evil of their deeds* (Jeremiah 23:18-22).

Remember that, as Jeremiah warned of destruction, others prophesied falsely of peace. God addressed the distortion by drawing a bright line between two kinds of messengers. Jeremiah was a true prophet who spoke under the unction of the Holy Spirit. He prophesied from the heart of God and was among those who stood in God's presence (His *Council*) and received His divine *counsel* (notice the homonyms and their spellings). The false prophets had not heard from God but prophesied anyway and deceived the people.

Let's examine the vocabulary for a moment. The word in verse 18 translated "council" in the New American Standard Bible is the Hebrew word *cowd,* which means "a session, i.e. company of persons (in close deliberation); by implication, intimacy, consultation, a secret."[1] Clearly, the explicit definition refers to a session or group; by extension, the word implies the *counsel* or guidance given by such a group. The distinction is important, but sometimes overlooked. For example, the King James Version translates *cowd* as "counsel"—not the convocation but its output (see Jer. 23:18,22 KJV).

Cowd also appears in Amos 3:7, where it is translated "secret":[2] *"Surely the Lord God does nothing unless He reveals His secret counsel to His servants the prophets."* Not only does God call and commission His prophets, but He also reveals His plans to them before He acts.

True prophets were brought into the Council of the Lord, the divine setting in which His eternal purpose was discussed and released for distribution through His chosen vessels. Yet, then as now, many prophesied from their own motives and understanding. Consider the soothsayer, Balaam, who prophesied for money. When *"Moab was in great fear because of* [Israel], *for they were numerous..."* (Num. 22:3) Balaam was hired to curse Israel (see Num. 22–23). Balaam was neither called nor commissioned by God; he had never been included in His Council. He was a false prophet who openly opposed God's eternal purpose. Fortunately, he was unable to curse God's people before the Moabite king; instead he blessed them profusely. Rarely do false prophecies end so well.

WARNING FOR TODAY

The warning Jeremiah delivered should speak loudly as it raises the issue of truth and accountability in prophecy.

Clearly, not all who prophesy are God-sent. Those who stand in His Council are motivated by His eternal purpose—nothing more and nothing less. Through godly discernment and fidelity to Scripture, we can distinguish the true from the counterfeit and remove false prophets from our midst.

The Council in Two Covenants

The Council of God is seen throughout Old and New Testament Scripture. Although the Council was "attended" by a select few under the Old Covenant, admission has been broadened under the New, as we will see. As you read the following descriptions, consider the details and the effect such encounters produce in those who experience them. We begin with a powerful description from the great prophet, Isaiah.

Isaiah

Isaiah's dramatic record from the Council includes a face-to-face encounter with God. In this exchange, God commissioned Isaiah to speak to a spiritually-hardened people. Isaiah proved to be fierce in his faithfulness to God's call. Put yourself in his shoes as you read and you will see how profoundly he was affected by his commissioning:

> *In the year of King Uzziah's death I saw the Lord sitting on a throne, lofty and exalted, with the train of His robe filling the temple. Seraphim stood above Him, each having six wings: with two he covered his face, and with two he covered his feet, and with two he flew. And one called out to another and said, "Holy, Holy, Holy, is the Lord of hosts, the whole earth is full of His glory." And the foundations of the thresholds trembled at the voice of him who called out, while the temple was filling with smoke.*
>
> *Then I said, "Woe is me, for I am ruined! Because I am a man of unclean lips, and I live among a people of unclean lips; for my eyes have seen the King, the Lord of hosts."*

Then one of the seraphim flew to me with a burning coal in his hand, which he had taken from the altar with tongs. And he touched my mouth with it and said, "Behold, this has touched your lips; and your iniquity is taken away and your sin is forgiven."

Then I heard the voice of the Lord, saying, "Whom shall I send, and who will go for Us?"

Then I said, "Here am I. Send me!" (Isaiah 6:1-8)

Isaiah lists several participants in this stunning encounter. We see the Lord seated on His throne, with the seraphim above Him. The remaining members of the Godhead are implied by the reference to *"Us"* in verse 8. In the midst of the scene is Isaiah, who was profoundly affected by what he saw and heard:

1.   He saw the Lord in His glory.

2.   He recognized his own uncleanness and was cleansed.

3.   He was made aware of the need for a prophet.

4.   He was commissioned to speak for the Triune God.

Isaiah was brought into the Council "room" of God. It was a key part of his commissioning in which he saw God's heavenly attendants and received understanding regarding God's plan for his life. The calling could not be clearer; the Council session produced a prophet who walked tall in his assignment, knowing that it had been issued by God Himself.

Ezekiel

Ezekiel had a similar experience. He described a specific day on which the Lord brought him into His Council: *"It came about in the thirtieth year, on the fifth day of the fourth month, while I was by the river Chebar among the exiles, the heavens were opened and I saw visions of God"* (Ezek. 1:1). Ezekiel saw the seraphim, which he described as "four living creatures," the eye-studded wheels that went with them, the throne of God, and the appearance of the Almighty (see Ezek. 1:5-28).

Once Ezekiel entered the Council of the Lord, he was commissioned:

> *Then He said to me, "Son of man, stand on your feet that I may speak with you!" And as He spoke to me the Spirit entered me and set me on my feet; and I heard Him speaking to me. Then He said to me, "Son of man, I am sending you to the sons of Israel, to a rebellious people who have rebelled against Me; they and their fathers have transgressed against Me to this very day"* (Ezekiel 2:1-3).

In the Council, Ezekiel was given the *counsel* of the Almighty, which he would deliver to Israel:

> *"Now you, son of man, listen to what I am speaking to you.... Open your mouth and eat what I am giving you." Then I looked, and behold, a hand was extended to me; and lo, a scroll was in it. When He spread it out before me, it was written on the front and back, and written on it were lamentations, mourning and woe.*

> *Then He said to me, "Son of man, eat what you find; eat this scroll, and go, speak to the house of Israel." So I opened my mouth, and He fed me this scroll. And He said to me, "Son of man, feed your stomach and fill your body with this scroll which I am giving you." Then I ate it, and it was sweet as honey in my mouth.*

> *Then He said to me, "Son of man, go to the house of Israel and speak with My words to them"* (Ezekiel 2:8–3:4).

Ezekiel was commanded to ingest the message (as was John the Beloved, in Revelation 10:9). In other words, the message became part of him. In keeping with the fact that the prophet *is* the message, he would suffer in order to bring it forth (see Ezek. 24:15-18). His trials served to temper him and empower him to speak, not just from the moment but from the eternal perspective that God desired His people to grasp.

Zechariah

The prophet Zechariah was present in the Council when satan brought accusation against the high priest, Joshua, who was dressed in filthy garments. God rebuked the accuser, and His Angel cleaned up the high priest:

> Next the Messenger-Angel showed me the high priest Joshua. He was standing before God's Angel where the Accuser showed up to accuse him. Then God said to the Accuser, "I, God, rebuke you, Accuser! I rebuke you and choose Jerusalem. Surprise! Everything is going up in flames, but I reach in and pull out Jerusalem!"
>
> Joshua, standing before the angel, was dressed in dirty clothes. The angel spoke to his attendants, "Get him out of those filthy clothes," and then said to Joshua, "Look, I've stripped you of your sin and dressed you up in clean clothes."
>
> I spoke up and said, "How about a clean new turban for his head also?" And they did it—put a clean new turban on his head. Then they finished dressing him, with God's Angel looking on.
>
> God's Angel then charged Joshua, "Orders from God-of-the-Angel-Armies: 'If you live the way I tell you and remain obedient in My service, then you'll make the decisions around here and oversee My affairs. And all My attendants standing here will be at your service'" (Zechariah 3:1-7 MSG).

Zechariah was made privy to the proceedings in God's Council *and* became a participant. When he suggested that a new turban be given to Joshua, the Council took his advice! God's Angel then informed Zechariah of the profound authority he had been given (pending his continued obedience) in order to fulfill God's commission. In essence God said, "I am calling you to be part of the Council."

Abraham

Abraham was an early "Council member" and God's friend (see Isa. 41:8; James 2:23). As such, God confided in him. Do you remember the three Visitors who came to Abraham at Mamre? After the patriarch and his wife, Sarah, provided a feast for their Guests, the couple was told about the son they would soon be granted by God. Just before Abraham and the Visitors parted, *"The Lord said, 'Shall I hide from Abraham what I am about to do, since Abraham will surely become a great and mighty nation, and in him all the nations of the earth will be blessed?'"* (Gen. 18:17-18). God included Abraham in His Council.

God then confided in Abraham His plans to destroy Sodom and Gomorrah (see Gen. 18:20-21; Amos 3:7). Like Zechariah, Abraham became an active participant in the Council. He boldly negotiated for the lives of Lot and his family. As a result, God promised to spare his loved ones from the destruction of the cities (see Gen. 18:23-32).

This wasn't Abraham's only experience in the Council. We saw in an earlier discussion that Abraham was made aware of Christ centuries before His advent. Jesus said, *"Your father Abraham rejoiced to see My day, and he saw it and was glad"* (John 8:56). Like Moses, Abraham was a Council "regular" who saw the Messiah's coming!

Moses

We have already seen much evidence of Moses' "membership" in the Council of the Lord. Exodus 33:11 says, *"The Lord used to speak to Moses face to face, just as a man speaks to his friend."* We know that Moses asked to see God's glory. Although God issued wise stipulations, Moses' request was granted! (See Exodus 33:18-23.) And in Exodus 24, Moses was invited to meet with God atop the mountain. "[God] *said to Moses, 'Come up to the Lord, you and Aaron, Nadab and Abihu and seventy of the elders of Israel, and you shall worship at a distance'"* (Exod. 24:1).

> *Then Moses went up with Aaron, Nadab and Abihu, and seventy of the elders of Israel, and they saw the God of Israel; and under His feet there appeared to be a pavement of sapphire, as clear as the sky itself. Yet He did not stretch out His hand against the nobles of the sons of Israel; and they beheld God, and they ate and drank* (Exodus 24:9-11).

Imagine yourself in this scene. Imagine the glory of it. Moses and his retinue were invited into the Council of the Lord and feasted there.

Paul and Nathanael

The Council of the Lord remains in session in post-ascension times. Consider Paul's account of what many scholars believe was his personal experience. In it, he mentions the *"inexpressible words"* heard in the Council:

> I know a man in Christ who fourteen years ago —whether in the body I do not know, or out of the body I do not know, God knows—such a man was caught up to the third heaven. And I know how such a man—whether in the body or apart from the body I do not know, God knows—was caught up into Paradise and heard inexpressible words, which a man is not permitted to speak. On behalf of such a man will I boast; but on my own behalf I will not boast, except in regard to my weaknesses (2 Corinthians 12:2-5).

The Council was not reserved for the most well-known among God's servants. One of Jesus' original disciples, Nathanael (who recognized Him as the Son of God the moment they met) received an invitation to the Council from Jesus Himself:

> Jesus saw Nathanael coming to Him, and said of him, "Behold, an Israelite indeed, in whom is no deceit!" Nathanael said to Him, "How do You know me?" Jesus answered and said to him, "Before Philip called you, when you were under the fig tree, I saw you." Nathanael answered Him, "Rabbi, You are the Son of God; You are the King of Israel." Jesus answered and said to him, "Because I said to you that I saw you under the fig tree, do you believe? You shall see greater things than these." And He said to him, "Truly, truly, I say to you, you shall see the heavens opened, and the angels of God ascending and descending on the Son of Man" (John 1:47-51).

Jesus promised Nathanael a front-row seat to the Council's proceedings.

The Body of Christ

Ephesians 2:6 says that Jesus *"raised us up with Him, and seated us with Him in the heavenly places, in Christ Jesus...."* In other words we, the Church of Jesus Christ, are called to the Council. Our invitation was telegraphed by Jesus when He told His disciples to expect the Holy Spirit:

> *But the Helper, the Holy Spirit, whom the Father will send in My name, He will teach you all things, and bring to your remembrance all that I said to you* (John 14:26).

> *John baptized with water, but you shall be baptized with the Holy Spirit not many days from now* (Acts 1:5).

> *You will receive power when the Holy Spirit has come upon you; and you shall be My witnesses both in Jerusalem, and in all Judea and Samaria, and even to the remotest part of the earth* (Acts 1:8).

The invitation was fulfilled on the Day of Pentecost. Since then, we have been seated in heavenly places—in the Council of the Lord:

> *And when the day of Pentecost had come, they were all together in one place. And suddenly there came from heaven a noise like a violent rushing wind, and it filled the whole house where they were sitting. And there appeared to them tongues as of fire distributing themselves, and they rested on each one of them. And they were all filled with the Holy Spirit and began to speak with other tongues, as the Spirit was giving them utterance* (Acts 2:1-4).

The Council takes on new meaning in the context of the born-again experience and the baptism of the Holy Spirit: No longer are a select few chosen; instead, the Holy Spirit indwells all—ascension gift or not. We are all invited to hear God's counsel; therefore we must bear responsibility to judge today's prophets and confirm that they speak only what they have heard in the Council of the Lord.

THE COUNCIL OF THE LORD IN OLD AND NEW COVENANTS

Isaiah	*"In the year of King Uzziah's death, I saw the Lord sitting on a throne, lofty and exalted, with the train of His robe filling the temple. Seraphim stood above Him, each having six wings: with two he covered his face, and with two he covered his feet, and with two he flew. And one called out to another and said, 'Holy, Holy, Holy, is the Lord of hosts, the whole earth is full of His glory'"* (Isaiah 6:1-3).
Ezekiel	*"Now it came about in the thirtieth year, on the fifth day of the fourth month, while I was by the river Chebar among the exiles, the heavens were opened and I saw visions of God"* (Ezekiel 1:1).
Zechariah	*"Then he showed me Joshua the high priest standing before the angel of the Lord, and Satan standing at his right hand to accuse him....Thus says the Lord of hosts, "If you will walk in My ways, and if you will perform My service, then you will also govern My house and also have charge of My courts, and I will grant you free access among these who are standing here""* (Zechariah 3:1,7).
Abraham	*"The Lord said, 'Shall I hide from Abraham what I am about to do, since Abraham will surely become a great and mighty nation, and in him all the nations of the earth will be blessed?'"* (Genesis 18:17-18). *"Your father Abraham rejoiced to see My day, and he saw it and was glad"* (John 8:56).
Moses	*"Then Moses went up with Aaron, Nadab and Abihu, and seventy of the elders of Israel, and they saw the God of Israel..."* (Exodus 24:9-10).
Paul	*"I know a man in Christ...such a man was caught up to the third heaven...whether in the body or apart from the body I do not know..."* (2 Corinthians 12:2-3).

THE COUNCIL OF THE LORD IN OLD AND NEW COVENANTS	
Nathanael	*"And He said to him, 'Truly, truly, I say to you, you shall see the heavens opened, and the angels of God ascending and descending on the Son of Man'"* (John 1:51).
Body of Christ	*"And when the day of Pentecost had come, they were all together in one place. And suddenly there came from heaven a noise like a violent rushing wind, and it filled the whole house where they were sitting. And there appeared to them tongues as of fire distributing themselves, and they rested on each one of them. And they were all filled with the Holy Spirit and began to speak with other tongues, as the Spirit was giving them utterance"* (Acts 2:1-4).

A Prophetic People

If the Church is God's prophetic instrument, we are His prophetic people. We are called to speak in the name of our Head, Jesus Christ, about what He has done, what He is doing, and what He is yet to do. A similar balance applies to the office of the prophet. Although foretelling is an important part of the prophet's call, it must not be his or her sole preoccupation. But know this: It is not solely up to the prophet to ensure balance and accuracy. Part of the Body's upward call is to detect whether the doma's ministry is sound.

The ultimate purpose of the New Testament prophet is to align the Church with God's eternal purpose. Both the prophets and the Body at large are called to be as intentional in this regard as God is. All prophetic speech, including the foretelling of events, is designed to reveal God's eternal purpose. We know foretelling is part of the prophetic equation because we see it in the Book of Acts (see Acts 5:9; 9:17, for example) and elsewhere (consider the Revelation). Scripture is our evidence of God's approval of the practice. Always, however, it is necessary to understand the measure of a particular prophet's rule in order to accurately appraise his or her prophetic conduct.

Abraham Joshua Heschel explains the purpose of foretelling from his Old Covenant perspective, which also applies in the New Covenant arena:

> The prominent theme is exhortation, not mere prediction. While it is true that foretelling is an important ingredient and may serve as a sign of the prophet's authority (Deut. 18:22; Isa. 41:22; 43:9), his essential task is to declare the word of God to the here and now; to disclose the future in order to illumine what is involved in the present.[3]

As a practical matter, it serves us well to follow the advice of Paul who said:

> *Let two or three prophets speak, and let the others pass judgment. But if a revelation is made to another who is seated, let the first keep silent. For you can all prophesy one by one, so that all may learn and all may be exhorted* (1 Corinthians 14:29-31).

In my opinion, Paul is saying that anyone can prophesy, but the prophecies must be judged rather than implicitly accepted by or on behalf of the congregation. With regret, I report that over the past 30 years or so, the Church has largely lost her footing in this area, leading to excesses that have served to hinder the Body's progress. In her current condition, she must first set the house in order and then return to a high level of operation in the revelatory gifts.

The Berean Mentality

To fully appreciate the finished work of the cross, function effectively as a faith community, and cast off counterfeits, we must understand our covenant. The first-century Bereans were exemplary in this regard. When Paul and Silas preached in their synagogue, they listened and searched out the Scriptures for themselves. Luke described them as being *"more noble-minded than those in Thessalonica, for **they received the word with great eagerness, examining the Scriptures daily, to see whether these things were so.** Therefore many of them believed, along with a number of prominent Greek women and men"* (Acts 17:11-12).

The Bereans did not receive Christ by whim and could not be *"tossed by every wind of doctrine"* (Eph. 4:14). They used their critical-thinking skills to test the words of the apostles and prophets. As a result, they were free to wholeheartedly embrace God's eternal truths.

PROPHETIC INSTABILITY

It is unfortunate that many who are not called as prophets and whose overall prophetic giftings are uncertain are quick to proclaim their inner impression as the voice of God. Often, what is speaking is not the Holy Spirit but wounded areas of the soul. Even the most thoughtful prophetic gatherings tend to attract those who are spiritually unstable. For the protection of these misguided "prophets" and those whom they affect, we must always judge prophetic activity with the help of the Holy Spirit, Church leadership, and the Word of God.

Rebuild the Prophetic Foundation

Part of the domain of the ascension gifts is to maintain continuity in the household of God. When gaps appear, whether doctrinally, functionally, spiritually, or otherwise, the doma gifts are called, under the anointing of God, to facilitate restoration. In the current age, this maintenance and restoration is part of the preparation of the Bride of Christ, who will come to the marriage supper of the Lamb in a spotless and wrinkle-free condition (see Eph. 5:27).

Prophets have served as gap-detectors throughout redemptive history. We saw Joshua's work in this area; he restored such a gap after the Israelites crossed the Jordan to take the Promised Land. Even as they followed the cloud by day and the pillar of fire by night, they lost sight of their essential covenantal bond of circumcision. Through Joshua's leadership, this element of their covenant was reinstated.

In our day and over the course of centuries, key elements of our covenant have been overlooked or discarded. Many have rejected what Jesus explicitly promised to His disciples when He said: *"John baptized with water, but you will be baptized with the Holy Spirit"* (Acts 1:5). In discarding this promise, they have also forfeited the giftings and power Jesus said would become available *"when the Holy Spirit has come upon you"* (Acts 1:8).

Such breaches in our prophetic foundation must be repaired for the Church to fulfill her role in the eternal plan of God!

> *Breaches in our prophetic foundation must be repaired for the Church to fulfill her role in the eternal plan of God!*

Foundation stones can become dislodged in any community. In the Body of Christ, the doma gifts, especially the apostles and prophets, are called to detect such damage, sound the alert, and see to the repairs. The longer such breaches remain, the more likely the Church is to create work-arounds such as complacency and tolerance toward the dysfunction. The further removed we become from God's intent, the greater will be our overall drift from His eternal purpose.

For wide swaths of today's Church, the prophetic foundation is found wanting. Doctrinal and denominational fissures have incited "family feuds" and fractured our ability to move as one Body (see Eph. 4:4). Some believe that prophets are anachronistic; therefore they prohibit manifestations of the Holy Spirit's prophetic giftings. (This approach often springs from a lack of understanding of Old and New Testament prophetic distinctions.)

For others, instability in the prophetic ranks has promoted widespread distrust. Reports of charlatans, false prophets, and other abuses causes cautious leaders (please note that caution is commendable) to judge *all* prophetic activity by errant standards. Rather than risk abuses, leaders play it "safe" and shun the doma gifts altogether. Instead of ensuring safety, such restrictions prevent the healthy growth of the Body and of individual believers whose God-given gifts (and destinies) are denied development.

On the other end of the spectrum are churches in which the realm of the prophetic is readily embraced, but a lack of leadership and accountability leads to dysfunction and confusion. Although some prophetic activity may provide benefit under these conditions, the damage done by parking-lot prophets, immature doma gifts, and reckless opportunists can be devastating.

Because the lack of a sound prophetic foundation can lead to generational drift and spiritual atrophy, the restoration of the foundation is critical. Through the anointing of the Holy Spirit, sound doctrine, a balanced approach to risk-taking and caution, and a willingness to mentor prophets and prophetic types, our foundation can be restored.

The Church can—and will—become the prophetic instrument God intended her to be.

The Spirit of Prophecy

As you know, the testimony of Jesus Christ is *the* message of the Church and the central passion of the prophet. According to the Revelation, it is the very spirit of prophecy. You will remember that when John fell down to worship an angel, the messenger said, *"Do not do that; I am a fellow servant of yours and your brethren who hold the testimony of Jesus; worship God. For the testimony of Jesus is the spirit of prophecy"* (Rev. 19:10).

Albert Barnes offers his view on this spirit of prophecy that is the testimony of Jesus Christ:

> The design of prophecy is to bear testimony to Jesus. The language does not mean, of course, that this is the only design of prophecy, but that this is its great and ultimate end. The word "prophecy" here seems to be used in the large sense in which it is often employed in the New Testament-meaning to make known the divine will....[4]

Remember the prophet's only message is Christ and ultimate purpose is to align the Church with God's eternal purpose (i.e., His divine will). The prophet's preoccupation fuels the vigilance with which he or she inspects and seeks to restore the prophetic foundation. The prophet desires the foundation to be set right so the Body can function in a manner reflective of Heaven. The prophet's cry is: *"on earth as it is in heaven"* (Matt. 6:10).

The spirit of prophecy is entirely Jesus-centered. As soon as Pentecost came to the 120, Peter was consumed with talking about Jesus. On that day, 3,000 were saved, and within days 5,000 more came into the Kingdom. When Paul was struck to the ground on the Damascus Road, he began preaching the testimony of Jesus. Isaiah said it this way: *"To the law and to the testimony! If they do not speak according to this word, it is because they have no dawn"* (Isa. 8:20).

A New Generation of Prophetic Voices

Wherever our prophetic foundation is lacking, and even where it flourishes, our continuity as a community demands the emergence of a new generation of prophetic voices. One of the greatest needs is for prophetic preaching—the kind that stirs the depths of the heart and makes Scripture come alive. It is the kind of preaching two men experienced on the road to Emmaus:

> *While they were talking and discussing, Jesus Himself approached, and began traveling with them. But their eyes were prevented from recognizing Him. And He said to them, "What are these words that you are exchanging with one another as you are walking?" And they stood still, looking sad* (Luke 24:15-17).

The two men, unaware that Jesus had joined them, went on to describe their heartbreak over His death and what they perceived as His failure to redeem Israel.

> *And He said to them, "O foolish men and slow of heart to believe in all that the prophets have spoken! Was it not necessary for the Christ to suffer these things and to enter into His glory?" Then beginning with Moses and with all the prophets, He explained to them the things concerning Himself in all the Scriptures* (Luke 24:25-27).

The men invited Jesus to stay the night. He accepted their hospitality and revealed His identity without a word:

When He had reclined at the table with them, He took the bread
and blessed it, and breaking it, He began giving it to them.
And their eyes were opened and they recognized Him; and He
vanished from their sight (Luke 24:30-31).

Immediately, the men *"said to one another, 'Were not our hearts burning*
within us while He was speaking to us on the road, while He was explaining
the Scriptures to us?'" (Luke 24:32).

Jesus' sermon on the road to Emmaus is the premier example of prophetic preaching. Once you have heard it, you are spoiled for anything less.
Not only do the Scriptures come alive under the anointing of a prophetic
preacher, but listeners' hearts come alive, too. Suddenly, a 2,000-year-old
text that was all too familiar becomes instead an existential word from the
existential Christ, who declares: *"This* is what I am saying to you and to the
Church, *now!"*

Prophetic preaching goes beyond mere prophesying; it brings revelation
and confirmation to the believer's heart. When a prophet opens the Book,
the Holy Spirit opens the soul, piercing the mind in such a way that you can
never see the Scriptures the same way again.

Clearly, this is what the Church desperately needs. The restoration of
prophetic preaching is the spiritual antidote to the quasi-spiritual "social
club" many call *church*. Such preaching will help restore the dynamics of the
early Church and past reformations. Watered-down messages will become
anathema and will be recognized as the slow-release spiritual poison they
are. The Church will regain the ability to deeply impact and utterly transform cultures.

Prophetic preaching demands a new kind of sermon preparation: the
kind that thrusts preachers to their knees to beseech the Holy Spirit. It is
time to ask Him, "What—*exactly what*—are You saying in this hour? Tell
me, and I will say it, too."

PROPHET PREACHING POWER

Prophetic preaching brings the human heart in direct connection with the divine. Distractions fall away, priorities are

realigned, and understanding is imparted. While this kind of preaching speaks to the heart of the individual, it is also relevant to the times, direction, state of affairs, and condition of the Church within the context of the current culture.

Time to Take Our Places

Then He said to me, "Son of man, eat what you find; eat this scroll, and go, speak to the house of Israel." So I opened my mouth, and He fed me this scroll. He said to me, "Son of man, feed your stomach and fill your body with this scroll which I am giving you." Then I ate it, and it was sweet as honey in my mouth. Then He said to me, "Son of man, go to the house of Israel and speak with My words to them" (Ezekiel 3:1-4).

In this hour, the Holy Spirit is holding out the Book anew, looking for a generation that will "take and eat." It is time to reacquaint ourselves with God's desire for the New Covenant Church. If we will eat the Book, His intent will become evident, the Body will function at the highest level, and the gifts will be about Christ alone. The salt and light we are called to be will bring transformation to our churches and to a world that is far from God and unaware of His glorious intent. His pure power will be manifested in the earth, lives will be changed, and miracles will be realized. The ultimate goal—perpetual revival—will become a reality.

All of this will spring from the Rock that is Christ.

This is not only a Church-wide goal; it is our individual mandate. When we become steeped in our community consensus, the Last Will and Testament of the Lord Jesus Christ, we will begin to recognize the mountains that stand tall with our names on them. Like Caleb, we will give notice to all squatters. We will enforce all eviction notices issued *"against the rulers, against the powers, against the world forces of this darkness, against the spiritual forces of wickedness in the heavenly places"* (Eph. 6:12) and we will take the territory that God empowered us to claim.

Pious platitudes cannot take us there. A partial Gospel will not suffice. Refusal to walk in the gifts God intended for us will ensure atrophy within the Body and continued degradation in the world beyond our pews. Every believer, apostle, prophet, and other Church leader must be willing to gore his or her sacred cows. It is time to set aside the distracting hum of familiarity and the tacit acceptance of predigested "manna." It is time to approach the Word of God with fresh ears, pure eyes, and a heart willing to compare every sermon to the Scriptures.

Now is the time to take our place in God's eternal plan. Our prophets must be willing to declare His truth without reservation. And we must determine that when God speaks, we will turn to hear His voice and obey. If we do, we will be positioned to make an eternal difference in the life of every person we meet for as long as we are graced to walk the earth.

This is the glorious mission of the household and army of God.

"And from the days of John the Baptist until now the kingdom of heaven suffers violence, and violent men take it by force" (Matthew 11:12).

Pinpoint the Prophetic

1. Based on our discussion and on your personal insights, describe the ways in which the call, both of prophets and believers at large, is an upward call.

2. Compare and contrast the Council of the Lord from Old and New Covenant perspectives.

3. Have you experienced prophetic foretelling? How did it affect you? How did it impact your life? How does it compare or contrast with other prophetic experiences you have had? If you have not experienced the prophetic, what is your response to all you have learned about it? How does it inform your perspective about faith in Christ?

4. Describe your relationship to the Church's prophetic foundation. What is your assessment of the foundation in your church experience? In what ways might you be called to facilitate its strengthening and/or restoration?

5. Where do you believe you are headed as a member of the household/army of God? How has your perspective been affirmed and/or modified while reading this book? What has God revealed to you about His plans for you and the Body of Christ?

The New Apostolic Reformation

And He who sits on the throne said, "Behold, I am making all things new." And He said, "Write, for these words are faithful and true" (REVELATION 21:5).

MORE THAN A DECADE AGO, THE WORLD CRINGED AT THE THOUGHT of Y2K. Experts predicted far-reaching technological calamity. Concerned citizens downloaded software patches and took other careful precautions. People everywhere were convinced that the new millennium would mean more than the turning of a calendar page.

Fortunately, Y2K was a fizzle. Yet the millennial change *was* significant. The world's transformed landscape testifies that it was. The acceleration and intensity of global activity is so striking that it speaks to something much deeper and more pervasive than the crises forming around us.

In the spirit realm, something has shifted—and everything is subject to change.

The "Shift Age"

The realities of 1999 are long gone. Today's world is far more complicated, distorted, and menacing. Yet despite the increasing darkness, evil will not define our future. We know that where sin abounds His grace abounds even more (see Rom. 5:20). And because He reminded us in advance, we know that God is *"making all things new"* (Rev. 21:5).

Many reliable prophetic voices have called the second decade of the new millennium a "shift age." I agree. I also believe that two critical groups are navigating the shift: One is an emerging company of God's faithful who have insight into the times. They choose to carry His light against the world's dark backdrop, doing exploits even they never imagined. The second group consists of masses of people paralyzed by oscillating waves of spiritual and natural activity that obscure truth, disorient populations, and breed mayhem.

Centuries ago, the prophet Daniel received revelation from a heavenly messenger who prophesied today's oscillating conditions:

> *But as for you, Daniel, conceal these words and seal up the book until the end of time;* **many will go back and forth,** *and knowledge will increase* (Daniel 12:4).

This dizzying back-and-forth motion is breeding distress worldwide. The world seems to have swung out of kilter. The evidence—in governments, economies, communities, and families—supports the perception. Our highly organized world *is* in disarray. Once-sturdy structures *are* crumbling. Darkness *has* shrouded the world. And entire populations brace for whatever is next.

Today's chaos resembles conditions *"in the beginning"* when *"the earth was formless and void"* (Gen. 1-2). But the Spirit of God is hovering over our swirling waters, ensuring the fulfillment of the Father's eternal purpose. The Bridegroom is poised for the continued unfolding of history, and His Bride is being readied for a new day.

Holy Discontent

God causes all things to work according to His ultimate intent and purpose. Regardless of whether we perceive His involvement, His unseen hand continues to move the heavens and the earth. Within the precise scope of

His will, He has brought us to this "shift age" and will lead us forward into a larger epoch.

The signposts point to the revolutionary leap in the Spirit that is already underway. It is happening in the realm of prophetic leadership *and* among the rank and file of committed believers. The clues are many: A holy season of discontent has begun. The spiritual status quo has lost its appeal. The chilling effects of political correctness are being cast off. Rote religious pursuits are being replaced with the relational intimacy God has always desired.

Serious Christ followers know that their radical commitment to Him is exactly what He wants. They have arrived at this conclusion in many different ways. Some have spent years foundering in neutral. Others have lived on the cutting edge their whole lives. Either way, they are determined to refute passivity and embrace risk for the sake of His cause.

The dissatisfaction with religiosity is a leading indicator that a revolution is already in progress. It is not fueled with angst or self-will. It is not contained in ugly words on placards. It is sustained by His Spirit, through grace. Its purpose is not change for its own sake.

He is not making *all new things;* He is making *all things new.*

Authentic Apostolic Culture

This "making new" includes the renewal and restoration of an emerging apostolic company to its archetype: the first-century Church. This was not a top-down organization run by a chosen few. It was the priesthood of all believers driven by the Great Commission to invade the culture with the love, compassion, and resurrection power of Christ.

As Isaiah prophesied, *"The government will rest on His shoulders..."* (Isa. 9:6). The apostolic culture is part of His government. Therefore it is inherently theocratic, resting on His shoulders rather than ours.

Now, after two thousand years of often worldly hierarchical development, it is time to give the Church of Jesus Christ back to its founder, for *His* purposes! Leaders will no longer find the latitude to polish and elevate their own interests. Instead, the self-serving will find themselves marginalized by God and replaced by genuine apostolic leaders.

This company is not for elitists who seek enthronement above the fray. Apostolic culture will be served by leaders who willingly take their positions at ground level to polish the saints and push *them* to the top. The saints will, in turn, transform the marketplace by revealing Christ.

The apostle Paul lived this model, as his work and writings reveal. His desire was for God's people to *"appear as lights in the world,"* even if it meant that he was *"poured out as a drink offering upon the sacrifice and service of* [their] *faith..."* (Phil. 2:15,17).

His Love...Our Compassion

For those who are determined to appropriate all that the Father has prepared for them, renewed intimacy with Him will result. The Father's love will become paramount in their thinking and motivation. Their ability to receive His love will empower them to also extend it. They will share the experience of Paul who said, *"The love of God has been poured out within our hearts through the Holy Spirit who was given to us"* (Rom. 5:5).

God's love will kindle in His people compassion for those living outside His Kingdom. In an age when the lost have downsized their dreams, the renewed saints of God will ramp up. As they pursue His dreams, their witness will touch the multitudes and bring Him glory. As society's structures fail, those who are clamoring for help and hope in the valley of decision will discover the Father of lights!

The compassion that springs from His heart is never helpless. It moved Jesus to heal the sick, deliver the oppressed, and raise the dead! It will require of us a deeper view of what it means to be spiritual. It will also shape our views of personal destiny around the Father's heart, which is to redeem. To the extent that we commit ourselves to His heart, we are fulfilled.

His compassion will also invigorate our evangelism. Outreach will not be done by committee but by a called-out company of believers who will boldly tell their personal stories. By being true witnesses of the light, they will reach those who have rejected dogma and tradition. They will find that even the hard-boiled soul is crying out (whether consciously or not) for a direct experience with Jesus Christ.

In the coming days, relationship will be the governing principle. The saints who press into greater intimacy with the Father will in turn be more open to intimacy with others. The importance of this intimacy cannot be overlooked, because relationship is the pipeline through which reformation travels.

Surrender keeps the pipeline flowing. When we lay down our interests, we can truly live for Him. We become free to serve others with the pure love that Jesus demonstrated.

Christ is coming to rule and reign in the hearts of the surrendered *for the sake of the lost.*

A New Wineskin

The new apostolic reformation cannot be contained in structures supported by the traditions of men. The old wineskin that is the institutional Church will not yield to reformation. It is rigid and resistant to prophetic voices.

The institutional Church has historically rejected what is ready to emerge in God's intent and purpose. This is not only true in the purely spiritual sense. Even Copernicus suffered the wrath of the Church's dogmatism when he claimed that the sun, and not the earth, was the center of our planetary system. And those who dared to read his theories did so under the threat of excommunication.

My point is that new wine requires a new wineskin (see Mark 2:22). As society becomes more secularized, saints who recognize the new wineskin will successfully carry His life beyond Church walls. In reality, God has always worked in the marketplace. However, the Church has resisted His ways. Too often, we have quarantined His presence and power within our walls. This is diametrically opposite to God's intent!

We are about to see a radical shift away from the Church as an institution in our culture toward the Church as a movement with the power to transform the culture. Christianity as an institution must die in order for Christianity as a transformational movement to be resurrected.

Through the process of death, burial, and resurrection, the Holy Spirit will make the wineskin new. This explains the fiery trials experienced by so many saints in recent years. It is what Peter described in his first epistle:

> *Beloved, do not be surprised at the fiery ordeal among you, which comes upon you for your testing, as though some strange thing were happening to you; but to the degree that you share the sufferings of Christ, keep on rejoicing, so that also at the revelation of His glory you may rejoice with exultation* (1 Peter 4:12-13).

Those who are privileged to share in Christ's sufferings also partake in the power of His resurrection. This deeper work of the Spirit is an earmark of the transition we have entered.

Mastering the Transition

This transition will force us to realize that we have prized our indoctrination more than we have valued a genuine experience with Christ. Unless and until we face this fact, we will perpetuate the old wineskin and the deadness it propagates. But be forewarned: the transition is upon us regardless of our willingness to accept it.

Mastery of the transition is critical to spiritual health, both individually and corporately. An upgraded skill set is needed to mount the learning curve. Among our improved skills is one that is counterintuitive to the natural mind: it is the decision to release ourselves from the Western perspective. This rational mind-set limits us to the intellectual assent to truth—even as we are headed into an age of the Spirit! In this age (and really since the Day of Pentecost) we have been called to operate *in, by,* and *with* the Spirit of God to achieve the Father's eternal purpose.

The Creation account helps us to understand the role of the Spirit in all that God does. *Before* God said, *"Let there be light"* (Gen. 1:3), the Spirit moved over the surface of the waters (see Gen. 1:2). The Spirit's prominent role was also seen when Jesus spoke to the woman at the well. He said, *"God is spirit, and those who worship Him must worship in spirit and truth"* (John 4:24). Jesus chose His words purposefully. He did not say "in truth and spirit," but *"in spirit and truth."*

What we know is of little consequence unless we *know Him.* Our beliefs are lifeless when they are detached from our relationship with the Spirit. Spirit and truth must be balanced. This is the balance Jesus struck perfectly when He ministered to people. Except when addressing the hypocrisy of the rigidly religious, Jesus never laid the weight of the law upon people without first revealing Himself and His love by the Holy Spirit.

The fields of harvest are ripe. Multitudes are oscillating in cycles of fear. They are sheep without a shepherd, and the Good Shepherd has called us to reach them—with His love.

Resurrection: A Way of Life

In the coming days, resurrection will be more than a doctrine. Doctrines will not speak to the hopeless; only life will draw them out of the darkness. Our consumer-driven culture has lost its attraction. Its foundations have been shaken. The hope once found in "things" is evaporating. The lost are asking, "Isn't there more to life than this?"

A renewed company of the elect will rise out of the dead things of our culture and *"press on toward the goal for the prize of the upward call of God in Christ Jesus"* (Phil. 3:14). They will not be the first generation to arise from a dead society into resurrection life. Instead they are being returned to the ancient patterns that first caused the Church to flourish in a hostile environment.

The pitfalls faced in the first century are similar to those of today. In the first case, powerful men in Judaism and the Roman Empire opposed the burgeoning Church. In many parts of our modern world, Christians live under the threat of death. In America, Christianity has been marginalized. Christians are depicted as quaint people who fail to grasp modern ideas. As a result, the beliefs they hold dear are savaged by government and media.

Yet this opposition does not signal defeat. Instead, I believe that hostility will serve as the backdrop for the greatest awakening since the 18th century! Springtime in the Spirit is coming to a generation willing to live radically for God.

Eternal Father, Eternal Son

The Father's love will be central to the committed Christian walk in the coming years. The concept of *Father* is central to divine purpose. We need to realize first of all that the Father is eternally the Father. He did not become the Father after His Son was manifested in the earth. Nor did the Son become the Son upon His Incarnation. He is eternally the Son. The Child had to be *born* for the plan of salvation to be fulfilled, but the Son *was given* (see Isa. 9:6).

Paternal love permeates God's eternal purpose. Just as the Father, who loves the Son and the world, seeks to bring many sons to glory (see Heb. 2:10), the Church must embrace the same purpose.

As His children, we are partakers in the divine intent. Isaiah 42:8 is commonly quoted by the "religious" to disqualify us from such a role. It says: *"I am the Lord, that is My name; I will not give My glory to another, nor My praise to graven images."*

Of course the Scripture is absolutely accurate; He will not give His glory to another. However, His children are not "another." We are His. We were made in His image and likeness (see Gen. 1:26). We are one with Him through Christ (see John 17:22). We are *in* Christ (see Rom. 8:1; 1 Cor. 1:30; Eph. 2:10). And Peter said we are *"partakers in the divine nature..."* (2 Pet. 1:4).

Because we partake in the divine nature, we also partake in His glory. This involves much more than the experience of His presence in a meeting of believers. His glory is the full actualization and expression of all He created us to be. When we fully actualize our destinies as He intended, He is glorified. Anything less misses His eternal purpose.

Father's House

Next-generation leaders called in this age will understand the Father's heart and make His intent theirs. Instead of being preoccupied with planning for the future, they will listen for His voice and replace their plans with His. Therefore, they will co-create, in collaboration with the Holy Spirit, the future that is about to emerge in the Father's eternal purpose.

This was Jesus' example. He did only what He saw the Father doing (see John 5:19). In this new apostolic reformation, we will be equally constrained. Good ideas will not suffice. Only God's ideas will pass muster. Church growth schemes, great programs, and beautiful buildings cannot substitute for adherence to the Father's leading.

The Church must be the Father's House. And in His house we must wear the garments He prepares—garments of love, compassion, reconciliation, grace, and mercy. These garments reflect the culture of Heaven. We wear them because we love the Father and are forever grateful to the Son!

We have been called by God *"into the fellowship of His Son..."* (1 Cor. 1:9 NKJV). This fellowship is the relationship enjoyed by the Son with the Father. Jesus described His intent for us to enter this fellowship:

> *I do not ask on behalf of these alone, but for those also who believe in Me through their word; that they may all be one; even as You, Father, are in Me and I in You, that they also may be in Us, so that the world may believe that You sent Me. The glory which You have given Me I have given to them, that they may be one, just as We are one; I in them and You in Me, that they may be perfected in unity, so that the world may know that You sent Me, and loved them, even as You have loved Me* (John 17:20-23).

Leadership and Eternal Purpose

To embody the new apostolic reformation is to follow Jesus' pattern. The agendas we saw as being proof of our good stewardship could very well be seen as chaff in God's eyes.

Paul explains:

> *No man can lay a foundation other than the one which is laid, which is Jesus Christ. Now if any man builds on the foundation with gold, silver, precious stones, wood, hay, straw, each man's work will become evident; for the day will show it because it is to be revealed with fire, and the fire itself will test the quality of each man's work* (1 Corinthians 3:11-13).

For the Church to become a world-revolutionizing movement, we must ask the Father what is in His heart. That is our only legitimate agenda. It is also the foundation of servant leadership, as modeled by the ultimate leader, Jesus Christ. As the Gospel of Matthew records: *"The Son of Man did not come to be served, but to serve, and to give His life a ransom for many"* (Matt. 20:28).

As we master this transition, mature leadership will be defined not by age but by attitude. Maturity will be seen as the solemn commitment to set aside self-interest, to serve the Father's purpose, and to cooperate with the Holy Spirit (who also serves God's eternal purpose):

> But when He, the Spirit of truth, comes, He will guide you into all the truth; for He will not speak on His own initiative, but whatever He hears, He will speak; and He will disclose to you what is to come (John 16:13).

An important distinction of Jesus' leadership model is often missed or misunderstood: Jesus did not serve people; He served the Father's purpose. Because of this pure motive, Jesus ended up serving people at a higher level than anyone before or since.

Jesus did not serve people; He served the Father's purpose. As a result, He served people at a higher level than anyone before or since.

Jesus' servant leadership extended past the plane of natural vision. His service was based on what He knew the Father was about to do—the thing that wanted to emerge from the Father's eternal purpose. Next-generation leadership will share Jesus' vision of service. They will work with whatever is ready to emerge from the eternal blueprint already inscribed on the Father's heart.

Reformation leadership is not sustained by knowledge. Ten laws for managers and eight ways to extreme success might be informative lessons. But at best they are leaves on the tree of the knowledge of good and evil. The kind of leadership we are being provoked to embrace draws only from the tree of life. The sap in that tree is encoded with the Father's DNA. When we draw from it, we can both anticipate and innovate from the standpoint of His thoughts.

Listening Power

God never planned for His people to be broadsided by what He had in mind. The prophet captures God's desire for us to be in the know, working with the Father rather than reacting to His movements: *"Behold, I will do something new, now it will spring forth;* **will you not be aware of it?** *I will even make a roadway in the wilderness, rivers in the desert"* (Isa. 43:19).

God's work, both in and through us, rests on His grace. Even in this He is purposeful. His grace is not meant to be squandered; it is designed to empower our cooperation with Him. Paul told the church at Corinth: *"Working together with Him,* **we also urge you not to receive the grace of God in vain..."** (2 Cor. 6:1). Eugene Peterson paraphrased the verse this way: *"Companions as we are in this work with you, we beg you,* **please don't squander one bit of this marvelous life God has given us"** (MSG).

The work of the Father is accomplished when we synergize with the Holy Spirit to birth what the Father has already declared. He is not asking for our commitment to *do, do, do,* but to *listen, listen, listen.* This is a New Covenant commitment in which performance is not revered. Instead, performance is the supernatural outflow of relationship and the communication that sustains it.

You probably remember that Jesus' first recorded miracle happened at a wedding feast. While the reception was in full swing, the wine ran out. When Jesus' mother Mary became aware of the problem, she solicited Jesus' help. He reluctantly got involved.

Notice what happened next: *"His mother said to the servants, 'Whatever He says to you, do it'"* (John 2:5). Jesus then instructed the servants. When He told them to fill the pots with water, they filled them. When He told them to take a sample to the headwaiter, they obeyed Him. (See John 2:6-8.) But here is the irony of the miracle: Nothing Jesus instructed seemed particularly relevant to the wine shortage issue. Yet the servants listened. It was their *listening* and not their *doing* that opened the door to the miracle.

The servants did not turn the water to wine. They simply cooperated with God's purpose and power. Jesus produced the hoped-for result. The same transforming power will be seen when we do what the servants did, which was to operate from His mind rather than their own.

Epoch of Reformation

The Father's clarion call is clear. The discontent in our ranks confirms it. We are entering an epoch of apostolic reformation in which the Church will be renewed, refreshed, and retooled for service. For those who are willing to let go of their institutional mind-sets, His ways will become their own. The top-down model of leadership we have accepted for too long will give way. Leaders will position themselves on the "bottom" so that others may be lifted up.

The chaotic environment surrounding us will not daunt us. It will be revealed as the canvas upon which God's creative power will be released. The lost and despondent will find hope as the Father's House becomes their own.

Being active participants in the manifestation of His glory will require us to understand where we are with God—not where we think we are or believe we ought to be but where we truly are. Then the glory of His grace will lead us into a new epoch of refreshing and restoration.

Peter's words to the newborn Church speak as pointedly to us as they did to first-century believers:

> *Therefore repent and return, so that your sins may be wiped away, in order that times of refreshing may come from the presence of the Lord; and that He may send Jesus, the Christ appointed for you, whom heaven must receive until the period of restoration of all things about which God spoke by the mouth of His holy prophets from ancient time* (Acts 3:19-21).

If we will listen, He will bring through us the fulfillment of all that He has declared!

A Closing Word...

My prayer is that you would continue to live in expectation of the brilliant things God has in store. May your relationship with Him be your bread, and may His life in you become manna to many. As you listen for His voice and obey, you will discover that He is already moving among those who have been excluded until now. They will not be left behind, because a courageous company is being prepared.

You are called to that company!

My heart is stirred like never before. His voice seems clearer than it has ever been. The sound of it is unmistakable! There is so much more ahead and so much more to share that another book is already in the making!

I look forward to sharing it with you...

Endnotes

Introduction

1. Walter Brueggemann, *The Prophetic Imagination,* 2nd ed. (Minneapolis, MN: Fortress Press, 2001), 21.

2. Dictionary.com, *Dictionary.com Unabridged*, Random House, Inc., s.v. "reductionism," http://dictionary.reference.com/browse/reductionism; accessed March 9, 2011.

Chapter 1

1. Although Walter Brueggemann and I do not share all views expressed in *The Creative Word,* his work is both thoughtful and informative. His discussion of Jeremiah 18:18 is of particular interest here.

2. Walter Brueggemann, *The Creative Word* (Philadelphia, PA: Fortress Press, 1982), 8.

3. Ibid.

4. Merriam-Webster Online, *Merriam-Webster Online Dictionary* 2011, s.v. "ethos," http://www.merriam-webster.com/dictionary/ethos; accessed March 16, 2011.

5. Brueggemann, 12.

6. Ibid., 12.

7. Ibid., 9.

8. Ibid.

9.   Merriam-Webster Online, *Merriam-Webster Online Dictionary* 2011, s.v. "pathos," http://www.merriam-webster.com/dictionary/pathos; accessed March 16, 2011.

10. Brueggemann, 12.

11. Ibid.

12. Abraham Joshua Heschel, *The Prophets: Two Volumes in One,* Vol. I (Peabody, MA: Hendrickson Publishers, 2010), 219.

13. Ibid., Vol. II, 2.

14. *Thayer's Greek Lexicon, Complete and Abridged formats,* Biblesoft, Inc. Electronic Database (© 2000, 2003), s.v. "logos."

15. *The World of Cyprus Greek-English Dictionary,* s.v. "logos," http://www .kypros.org/cgi-bin/lexicon; accessed March 17, 2011.

16. Brueggemann, 9.

17. Ibid., 10.

18. Ibid., 12-13.

19. Biblesoft's New Exhaustive Strong's Numbers and Concordance with Expanded Greek-Hebrew Dictionary. CD-ROM. Biblesoft, Inc. and International Bible Translators, Inc. (© 1994, 2003, 2006) s.v. "Bezalel," (OT 1212).

20. Ibid., s.v. "Aholiab," (OT 171).

21. *Blue Letter Bible,* "Dictionary and Word Search for *doma* (Strong's 1390)," 1996-2011, < http:// www.blueletterbible.org/lang/lexicon/ lexicon.cfm?Strongs=G1390&t=KJV >; accessed March 18, 2011.

Chapter 2

1.   *Blue Letter Bible,* "Dictionary and Word Search for *chephets* (Strong's 2656)," 1996-2011, http://www.blueletterbible.org/lang/lexicon/ lexicon.cfm?Strongs=H2656&t=KJV; accessed April 26, 2011.

2.   Dictionary.com, *Dictionary.com Unabridged*, Random House, Inc., s.v. "intent," http://dictionary.reference.com/browse/intent; accessed: March 21, 2011.

3. Adam Clarke, *Clarke's Commentary,* Electronic Database, (© 1996, 2003, 2005), Biblesoft, Inc., s.v. "Matt. 4:4."

4. Ibid.

5. Ibid.

6. Biblesoft's New Exhaustive Strong's Numbers and Concordance with Expanded Greek-Hebrew Dictionary, CD-ROM, Biblesoft, Inc. and International Bible Translators, Inc. (© 1994, 2003, 2006) s.v. "pleroo," and "pleroma" (NT 4137 and 4138).

7. Dictionary.com, *Dictionary.com Unabridged*, Random House, Inc., s.v. "replete," http://dictionary.reference.com/browse/replete; accessed March 25, 2011.

8. Dictionary.com. *Dictionary.com Unabridged*, Random House, Inc., s.v. "complete," http://dictionary.reference.com/browse/complete; accessed March 25, 2011.

9. Karl Ellinger and Wilhelm Rudolph, editors, *Biblia Hebraica Stuttgartensia,* 5th revised ed., Adrian Schenker, ed., (Deutsche Bibelgesellschaft Stuttgart, 1977 and 1997) PC Study Bible Formatted Electronic Database, Biblesoft, Inc., (1988, 2003, 2006), s.v. "Ps. 118:22."

10. Biblesoft's New Exhaustive Strong's, s.v. "pinnah," (OT 6438).

11. Merriam-Webster Online, *Merriam-Webster Online Dictionary 2011,* s.v. "bulwark," http://www.merriam-webster.com/dictionary/bulwark; accessed March 25, 2011.

12. Merriam-Webster Online, *Merriam-Webster Online Dictionary 2011,* s.v. "tower," http://www.merriam-webster.com/dictionary/tower?show=0&t=1301082616; accessed March 25, 2011.

Chapter 3

1. Adam Clarke, *Clarke's Commentary,* Electronic Database, (© 1996, 2003, 2005), Biblesoft, Inc., s.v. "Eph. 4:8."

2. Ibid.

3. *Blue Letter Bible,* "Dictionary and Word Search for *laqach* (Strong's 3947)," 1996-2011, < http:// www.blueletterbible.org/lang/lexicon/ lexicon.cfm?Strongs=H3947&t=KJV >; accessed March 26, 2011.

4. Biblesoft's New Exhaustive Strong's Numbers and Concordance with Expanded Greek-Hebrew Dictionary, CD-ROM, Biblesoft, Inc. and International Bible Translators, Inc. (© 1994, 2003, 2006) s.v. "laqach," (OT 3947).

5. *Blue Letter Bible,* "Dictionary and Word Search for *doma* (Strong's 1390)," 1996-2011, < http:// www.blueletterbible.org/lang/lexicon/ lexicon.cfm?Strongs=G1390&t=KJV >; accessed March 18, 2011).

6. Ibid.

7. Dictionary.com, *Dictionary.com Unabridged,* Random House, Inc., s.v. "temperament," http://dictionary.reference.com/browse/temperament; accessed March 28, 2011).

8. Merriam-Webster Online, *Merriam-Webster Online Dictionary 2011,* s.v. "genius," http://www.merriam-webster.com/dictionary/genius; accessed March 29, 2011).

Chapter 4

1. Biblesoft's New Exhaustive Strong's Numbers and Concordance with Expanded Greek-Hebrew Dictionary, CD-ROM, Biblesoft, Inc. and International Bible Translators, Inc. (© 1994, 2003, 2006) s.v. "send," (NT 649).

2. Ibid., s.v. "send," (OT 7971).

3. *Blue Letter Bible,* "Dictionary and Word Search for *shalach* (Strong's 7971), 1996-2011, < http://www.blueletterbible.org/lang/lexicon/ lexicon.cfm?Strongs=H7971&t=KJV >; accessed March 30, 2011.

4. Dictionary.com, *Dictionary.com Unabridged,* Random House, Inc., s.v. "viscera," http://dictionary.reference.com/browse/viscera; accessed: March 30, 2011.

5. Merriam-Webster Online, *Merriam-Webster Online Dictionary 2011,* s.v. "visceral," http://www.merriam-webster.com/dictionary/visceral; accessed March 30, 2011.

6. Biblesoft's New Exhaustive Strong's, s.v. "proton," (NT 4412).

Chapter 5

1. Eric Charles White, *Kaironomia: On the Will-to-Invent*, (Ithaca, NY: Cornell UP, 1987), 13, as quoted in "Kairos," A Journal for Teachers of Writing in Webbed Environments, http://www.technorhetoric.net/ layers/metaphor.html; accessed April 5, 2011.

2. *Blue Letter Bible*, "Dictionary and Word Search for *kairos* (Strong's 2540)," 1996-2011, < http:// www.blueletterbible.org/lang/lexicon/ lexicon.cfm?Strongs=G2540&t=KJV >; accessed April 5, 2011.

3. Jack W. Hayford, ed., *Spirit-Filled Life Bible NKJV* (Nashville: Thomas Nelson, Inc., 1991), margin note for Exod. 3:3.

4. Biblesoft's New Exhaustive Strong's Numbers and Concordance with Expanded Greek-Hebrew Dictionary, CD-ROM, Biblesoft, Inc. and International Bible Translators, Inc. (© 1994, 2003, 2006) s.v. "metanoia," (NT 3341).

5. *Blue Letter Bible*, "search for *metanoeō* (Strong's 3340)," < http:// www .blueletterbible.org/lang/lexicon/lexicon.cfm?strongs=G3340 >; accessed April 5, 2011.

Chapter 6

1. Walter Brueggemann, "The Prophetic Imagination," The New York Avenue Presbyterian Church, http://www.nyapc.org/docs/ brueggemann/propheticimagination.pdf; accessed April 7, 2011.

2. David S. Dockery, general editor, *Holman Bible Handbook* (Nashville, TN: Holman Bible Publishers, 1992), 423.

3. "The Declaration of Independence," *National Archives,* http://www .archives.gov/exhibits/charters/declaration_transcript.html; accessed April 7, 2011.

4. Walter Brueggemann, "The Prophetic Imagination."

5. Ibid.

6. Ibid.

7. Merriam-Webster Online, *Merriam-Webster Online Dictionary 2011,* s.v. "insight," http://www.merriam-webster.com/dictionary/insight; accessed April 8, 2011.

8. Ibid., s.v. "intuition," http://www.merriam-webster.com/dictionary/intuition?show=0&t=1302232887; accessed April 8, 2011.

9. BrainyQuote, "Albert Einstein Quotes," http://www.brainyquote.com/quotes/quotes/a/alberteins165188.html; accessed April 8, 2011.

10. Ibid., "Lying Quotes," http://www.brainyquote.com/quotes/keywords/lying_8.html; accessed April 8, 2011.

Chapter 7

1. Abraham Joshua Heschel, *The Prophets: Two Volumes in One,* Vol. 1 (Peabody, MA: Hendrickson Publishers, 2010), 26.

2. Walter Brueggemann, *The Prophetic Imagination,* 2nd ed., (Minneapolis, MN: Fortress Press, 2001), 14.

3. Heschel, 26.

4. Ibid., 24.

5. Ibid., 25.

6. Ibid.

7. Ibid.

8. Ibid., 5.

9. Ibid., 25.

10. Ibid., 25-26.

Chapter 8

1. Herbert Lockyer, Sr., ed., *Nelson's Illustrated Bible Dictionary* (Nashville: Thomas Nelson Publishers, 1986), s.v. "Moses."

Chapter 10

1. Gamaliel was the "grandson of the famous rabbi Hillel." M. G. Easton, *Illustrated Bible Dictionary,* 3rd ed (Harper & Brothers, 1903), PC

Study Bible formatted electronic database, Biblesoft Inc., (© 2003, 2006), s.v. "Gamaliel."

2. Adam Clarke, *Clarke's Commentary,* Electronic Database, (© 1996, 2003, 2005), Biblesoft, Inc., s.v. "Acts 9:5."

3. Herbert Lockyer, Sr., ed., *Nelson's Illustrated Bible Dictionary* (Nashville: Thomas Nelson Publishers, 1986), s.v. "Paul."

Chapter 11

1. Warren W. Wiersbe, *The Bible Exposition Commentary/Prophets* (Colorado Springs: Cook Communications, 2002), s.v. "Zech. 4:4-7."

Chapter 12

1. Biblesoft's New Exhaustive Strong's Numbers and Concordance with Expanded Greek-Hebrew Dictionary. CD-ROM. Biblesoft, Inc. and International Bible Translators, Inc. (© 1994, 2003, 2006) s.v. "cowd," (OT 5475).

2. Ibid.

3. Abraham Joshua Heschel, *The Prophets: Two Volumes in One,* Vol. I (Peabody, MA: Hendrickson Publishers, 2010), 12.

4. Albert Barnes, *Notes on the New Testament* (London: 1884-1885, Blackie & Sons), Blackie & Son, London, 1884-85, Electronic Database (© 1997, 2003, 2005), Biblesoft, Inc., s.v. "Rev. 19:10."

About Mark Chironna

CERTIFIED LIFE COACH, PUBLIC SPEAKER, AUTHOR, AND PASTOR, Dr. Mark Chironna bridges the intellectual and spiritual realms to dismantle emotional barriers, empower lives, and release the creativity and personal power of the individual. His authentic and compassionate approach has transformed lives through one-on-one mentoring, speaking engagements, print, and electronic media.

IN THE RIGHT HANDS, THIS BOOK WILL CHANGE LIVES!

Most of the people who need this message will not be looking for this book. To change their lives, you need to put a copy of this book in their hands.

> *But others (seeds) fell into good ground, and brought forth fruit, some a hundred-fold, some sixty-fold, some thirty-fold* (Matthew 13:8).

Our ministry is constantly seeking methods to find the good ground, the people who need this anointed message to change their lives. Will you help us reach these people?

> *Remember this—a farmer who plants only a few seeds will get a small crop. But the one who plants generously will get a generous crop* (2 Corinthians 9:6).

EXTEND THIS MINISTRY BY SOWING
3 BOOKS, 5 BOOKS, 10 BOOKS, OR MORE TODAY,
AND BECOME A LIFE CHANGER!

Thank you,

Don Nori Sr., Founder
Destiny Image
Since 1982